Man

Up!

One Man's Sincere Regret for Sabotaging His Relationships

Derrick Taylor
DTaylorbooks.com

Man
Up!

ONE MAN'S SINCERE REGRET for SABOTAGING HIS RELATIONSHIPS

DTAYLOR Books™

ATLANTA, GA

Published by *DTAYLOR Books*™

Man Up: One Man's Sincere Regret for Sabotaging His Relationships

Copyright © 2011 by Derrick Taylor

Cover Design © 2011 by BCCM

All rights reserved. No part of this publication may be reproduced or transmitted in any form or by any means, including informational storage and retrieval systems, without permission in writing from the copyright holder, except for brief quotations in a review.

DTaylor Books may be purchased for educational, business, or sales promotional use. For information please right: Special Market Departments, DTaylor Books Publishers, P.O. Box 77871, Atlanta, GA 30357.

FIRST EDITION

ISBN 978-1-61364-382-2
LCCN 2011909320

DTAYLOR Books™ publishing, printing, 2011

To every woman who has been a part of my life and felt that I've done her wrong, I apologize.

This book is dedicated to my grandmother, Mrs. Arnelia Taylor, and to my uncle Mr. Carl Taylor, may they rest in peace. To my mother Mrs. Mary Taylor, to my sister Mrs. Shannon Taylor-Bell, and to my brothers Mitch Taylor, Israel Lee, and Terry Taylor. Last but not least, to my son Caleb Taylor, whom I love with all my heart.

Contents

Introduction
I Had to Man Up   1

———————

1 **My Disrespectful Intentions** 7

2 **The Games I Played** 17

3 **Product of My Environment** 31

4 **My Youth Development** 47

5 **Short of My Expectations** 67

6 **A Walk in My Shoes** 81

7 **My Lack of Ambition** 89

8 **Life Is What I Made It** 117

9 **My Brother's Keeper** 133

10 **Forever In My Heart…R.I.P. 143**

11 **I Am All Grown Up 153**

12 **The Conversation About Men and Women 159**

13 **Let's Blog: The Answers to Your Questions 169**

14 **Your Approach Determines Your Place 177**

15 **Let Your Intuition Guide You 169**

Book Review: What Are Your Thoughts? 183

Acknowledgements 185

About The Author 187

Afterword 191

I Had To Man Up

> *If a child lacks proper structure and guidance and doesn't see in their family life how to treat and respect the opposite sex they grow up with a distorted view of relationships in general-they are raised not knowing how to return love.*
>
> *~D. Taylor*

I lived most of my adult life thinking I was the ideal gentleman and God's gift to women. My arrogance and conceitedness led me to believe that I was a responsible and caring man who people could depend on. I discovered during my journey here on God's earth, it is this: (a) many women like acknowledgement, and loving affection from men, (b) women want men they can trust and be able to discuss problems they may be acquiring without difficulties, (c) I've lacked these qualities for many years.

Derrick Taylor

I know this because every relationship I tried to have I sabotaged it. I looked back on my relationships and have asked myself many times how a woman can ever obtain respect, love, and adoration if there are people like me who act like men, but in reality are not men at all. A sincere man will not viciously tear down the women who care for him. When dealing with women I had to be in control. I was immature, led by sexual intent, and extremely self-centered.

This is what I wish for the readers of *Man Up: One Man's Sincere Regret for Sabotaging His Relationships*. First I want every woman to know if a man is not treating and respecting you as he should that man is not the one for you, and you should not keep yourself in that situation. I want women who are in a relationship or involved with a man to see if her man has these behaviors that I discuss. Second, I want every man who may have these behaviors I speak of to know that these behaviors are not tolerated, and men should not disrespect or degrade women. Most importantly, I want men and women to seek positive relationships and let the dream of marriage become their goal. I did not have that family-oriented bond, which consists of a mother and a father in the same household but I know how important it can be if you are a part of one.

As I reflect back on my life, I can see how my upbringing shaped my disrespectful behavior toward women. I have thought about all the relationships that I've had and ask myself why it is so difficult to build a long-term, loving, and respectful relationship with a woman. In this book lie the answers to my questions that I want to share with you. I allow you into my mindset to better understand me maturing and becoming a man.

I Had to Man Up!

Man Up!

My Disrespectful Intentions

Chapter 1

My Disrespectful Intentions

> *I'm writing about my experiences and behavior towards women, in hopes of helping men who have traveled the same path, gone a relatable distance, and journeyed along a similar road. Given the power of evolution, I've become a better person and realized that this very book can help them do the same.*
>
> *~D. Taylor*

1

My Disrespectful Intentions

In my life, I've found tremendous disappointment in the way I have treated people, especially women! From preying on women and taking advantage of the weak to verbal and physical disrespect, my attitude and outlook has contributed to a cycle of outlandish behavior that revealed a glimpse of me, that you'd never care to see. I believe such demons surface from my controlling ways and that is just a selfish behavior for a man. Whatever the case or cause, little progress toward significant change has occurred over the years.

Today it is clear to me that I was acting in a way that went against what my mother instilled in me. However, inherited bad habits and views on women justified my actions and supported my thoughts-***women don't deserve my re-***

spect. Of course there has been plenty of backlash on how I dealt with women, but my firm stance on it made me care very little about the thoughts of others.

> **As a young adult, things a woman could do for me were limited to:**
> - **Sex.**
> - **Gifts.**
> - **The flexibility to be available on my terms.**

It wasn't their fault that I treated them so carelessly. I did it because I never trusted myself, much less them. I was caught up in a life of betrayal and dishonesty. I can't recall telling a woman the truth. I assumed that they deserved the lies I was telling them. From my understanding women lied too, and my objective was to beat them to it. To be honest, my mindset was that I was not going to respect them. Then again, I never actually took the time to get to know those women. I just didn't want to invest the time.

I never had a steady relationship. I have had different women in and out of my life. When I noticed them beginning to develop feelings, I would end the relationship and begin a new affair with someone else. I refused to get caught up with one woman. If I found myself spending too much time with the same girl I would quickly distance myself. Truthfully, I can count on one hand how many women I have genuinely cared for in my life, three. The sad thing about that was I could not even make it work out with the only three women I cared about. The reason for that was quite simple:

> **I was immature and still wanted to play games.**

I would sabotage the situation before it progressed because I constantly lied about everything. I only cared about the sex, and the women could only be useful when they did things that would benefit me. I always cheated, sharing my time with other girls. It became a cycle that I repeated no matter who I was involved with.

Sad, but the fact of the matter was that somebody had to be made a fool, and it wasn't going to be me. I had the attitude that I was too smooth and too much of a big-time player to have just one woman. My craving was sex and more sex when it came to women. Which I had plenty of in my life. Sometimes I feel ashamed when I reflect back on my experience. **The more women I could sleep with the better.**

*****

Derrick's Truth: In high school my friends and I played immature games with girls, one of our favorites being to see how many pairs of panties we could collect from everyone we slept with. We would have sex with as many girls as we could and afterwards leave with their panties. I remember hiding shoeboxes full of their garments in my closet as if I ran a lingerie store.

*****

Women who were a part of my life thought they shared a bond with me. They did, but not in a relationship way. I was clearly only in it for sex and money. If a woman wanted to spend time with me it had to be on my terms. It had to be a day I chose and at the time I awarded them. I only cared about the value of my time, not respecting how valuable their time was. In any situation it was my way or the highway. Sometimes I would make it clear what a woman was there for when she came to see me. About 90 percent of the time I spent with women was during what is known as "booty-call" hours. I would be out all day with my friends and when I had the urge to be with a woman, I would give her that late-night call. If she did come over and didn't do what I wanted her to do, I would kick her out saying, "I had to be at work early", or I would have one of my boys call and make it seem that I had to go pick them up, forcing her to leave. It did not matter what time it was. After she would leave, I would phone the next girl with whom I had a better chance to get the sex that I wanted.

I had my standards when it came to the type of women I would be seen with. I had my above-average and my average. The above-average women had every physical attribute I liked. They had the look, the body, and the attitude (someone like an Alicia Keys type woman). The women I stereotyped as my average women may not have had the look that I was attracted too, but had the body, (someone like an Omarosa type woman).

Behind closed doors, it was whatever I thought was necessary with the average women. I knew it was wrong to mess with these women, but I just didn't care. It was bad enough that they could not get a decent man; I was making it even harder for them to trust any man. ***I believed a woman was always beneath me***. To make it plain and simple, I wasn't the type of person who liked to get involved with someone past a certain point. My disrespectful intentions had to change.

MORAL

In this chapter I admit that I was a selfish and disrespectful man toward women. Today what I notice about some men is that they do not take the time to get to know women for whom they are and to see the good in them. They want everything that comes with a relationship except the commitment. Every woman is different and unique in her own way. Too many women make it easy for the fellas, but instead need to make it more of a challenge. In other words, women stop accepting the disrespectful behavior from men and men stop taking women for granted.

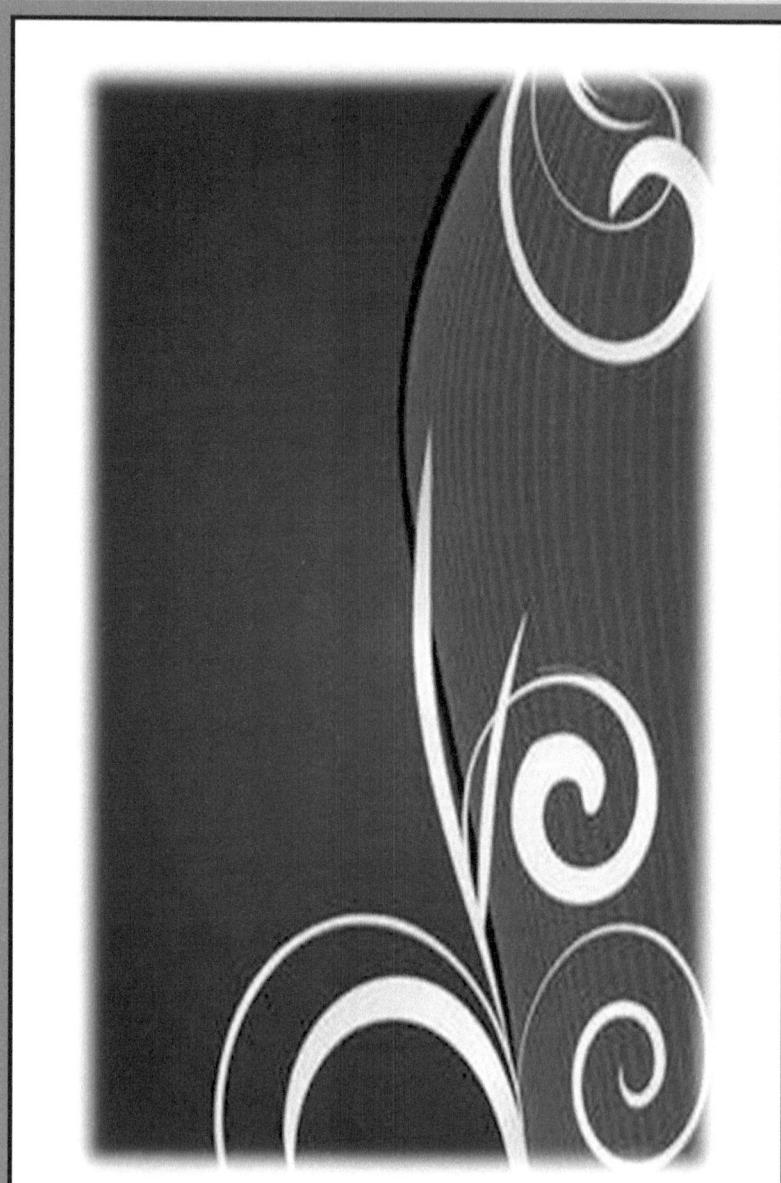

Man Up!

The Games I Played

Chapter 2

The Games I Played

> *Women like acknowledgement and loving affection. They want a person with whom they can relate. They want a person they can trust. They want to be able to discuss problems they might be having, without difficulties. Women are mysterious, but they will show you what it feels like to be truly loved, as long as you're willing and able to accept the responsibility of a true loving relationship. You have to show them and mean it, no matter how hard it may be for you at the time. Women like men who are compassionate and understanding and someone who always genuinely cares. A woman wants a man to tell her often how important she is to him and show her that in his actions.*
>
> *~D. Taylor*

2

The Games I Played

I can admit today that in the past my approach to dating women was very manipulative. My motives were unsuspected because I was a charmer. I had a good "talk-game" as the fellas would say. The following applied to my approach:

- **I had a way of making women I dated fell comfortable by showing interest in everything they liked and by coming off as I am a great listener. I made sure that they thought chivalry wasn't dead.**
- **I presented myself trustworthy by including them into my circle when I would hang out.**
- **My attitude around them was always funny and entertaining.**

With decent looks, charm, and the above I had women feeling as if I could be the one. They would have such a memorable time with me and start to think, "Hey this guy isn't so bad." As the saying goes, *"Everything is peaches and cream,"* in the beginning.

It was not long after I would meet a young lady before engaging sex. My favorite line was how I would tell women I haven't been sexually involved for months and that I was trying to wait until I found the right girl or until I was married (of course I wasn't looking for either of those things). My goal was to make her feel that I cared about her. ***I wasn't looking for the right-girl I was looking for the right-now girl*.**

All I required was the belief that they could trust me. The worst of it was that after sex it did not matter whether or not it was good for her; I was pleased to have accomplished the goals I had set for myself. I always knew that I was never going to see those women again. I created a list where I would write down all the names of the women I was sleeping with just to keep track of how many there actually were. My approach was the same whenever I wanted to attract a woman "if not broken, don't fix it." It became so easy to tell a woman what she wanted to hear that it made my chances of being with her effortless. My behavior was out of control and there was no turning back.

Women say all the time that they cannot find a good man. When they found me they certainly weren't receiving a good man. I had never been in a relationship that meant anything to me. To the women it meant a lot. The sole purpose of any relationship I had was to fulfill my needs and desires. My relationships never had anything to do with the other person. I was very unpredictable and had this mystery about me that women could not figure out. I always played a great deal and loved to say things like, "I am seeing another girl", and when they would get upset I would say that I was just playing; but I wasn't. It would leave them without a clue on what to believe.

I knew that women loved to express themselves, that is their nature, but when I would converse with them I did not care about them expressing how they felt, what they were thinking, or how their day was. Our conversations would always turn out to revolve around me. If it wasn't about me it was a waste of time. I was never a good listener and my attention span was even shorter. I had become this out-of-control sex addict. Sex became the first and only thing on my mind when I was around a woman. Some women accepted this behavior because I knew they lacked self-esteem, and some women didn't. I wanted nothing to do with those who did not accept it. They were a waste of my time.

The main reason I haven't had many relationship was because I was very picky. If the women did not have that exotic superficial look about them, I was not interested. The type of women I was interested in had light complexion and long natural hair, and they were very petite (a model-type woman, like those seen in music videos). In bed, they had to have a freaky side because I was a freak myself. My brother always used to tell me that I was color struck and he wasn't wrong. If she was not lighter than me I just wasn't that interested, especially in a relationship kind of way.

I lost several connections with women because I was never the romantic type. Holding hands with a woman in public was not an option. I was very disrespectful in public when I was with a woman. I had wandering eyes that checked out every woman I saw and I did not try to hide it.

The Games I Played

I was very rude indeed. Even when I was dating a woman, when the summer season came, I would break up with her just to catch the next fling that was out there. I rarely kept something serious with a woman around the summer season. During that time I would feel as though I was missing out on something, so I would never commit.

I always thought the grass was greener on the other side. My problem was that I never took the time to explore whether or not any of these women I met were a great fit for me. I never took the time to get to know them like I should have. I was too far gone trying to keep this bad-boy, player image. Eventually, I started feeling bad about my behavior. What I was doing was putting the exclamation mark on the stereotype that women already held which is that all men are dogs. Raised by a single mother and growing up with one sister, one would think I'd have more respect for women. I should have learned to be a respectful man toward women from seeing how men treated both my mother and sister. I was even worse than those men. I lacked knowledge on how to treat women; lying to them was what I knew best. I could be talking to a woman and know immediately, before we had a conversation that I was going to lie. The reason being:

> - **It was easy, and I could lie myself into anything.**
> - **If I was interested, I lied because I feared she wouldn't be interested in the truth.**

My problem was that I blamed all women I was involved with for any wrongdoing in our relationship. Compromising was not an option, basically, "I meant what I said and that's what was going to happen." I wasn't a very understanding person. A man pursues a woman in hopes that he will bond and one day get to the point of having a family. I was never thinking about a family or what it took to have one, I didn't grow up that way. Sometimes I would even intrude on other people's relationships. If I saw any signs that a woman was interested that was my opportunity to take advantage of the situation. It became a challenge for me to take other men's women. Knowing it was wrong did not bother me. I had to have what I wanted. Married women were no exception. I thought I was helping them out by attempting to satisfy their needs. I had my fair share of trysts with married women. I did not care if she was committing adultery; because that wasn't my problem

Breaking up a happy home was not my concern. I never thought about karma, or how it would feel to have a wife who was cheating on me. Because I wasn't in that situation, it was of no concern. I was a part of her infidelity. There was no doubt in me that I had to accomplish the goal of interfering in their relationship just to prove to myself that I still had game. The majority of the time I was successful, and sometimes I was not. When I wasn't, I would not give up. I hardly ever take a woman on a date, especially if I were only pretending to like her or wasn't interested in them. If we did go out, most of the time they would pay, I would only pay for something when I knew I would get something in return. I never liked to be with a woman in public. I did not want to take the chance of running into another woman with whom I was also involved. I hardly ever called a woman during respectable hours. If she didn't mean anything to me, she did not have the luxury of getting that kind of respect from me.

Derrick Taylor

My sexual appetite was very high. I have enjoyed many one-night stands. If a woman was not putting out, she was of no interest to me for any longer than that night. It did not help that I was living in Atlanta, a city that was known for having many beautiful single women, and where women outnumbered men. I had women all over town. I hate to admit, it was funny to me how many numbers I'd get and how many choices I had to make when it came down to me calling a certain type of women. I had labels for the women I associated with:

- **Miss Breadwinner: the woman who would give me material things because financially she could afford to.**
- **Head: the woman who only gave me oral satisfaction; who I didn't want to sleep with.**
- **In-House: the woman I could call on for sex anytime, no matter what the situation because that's all she was used for.**

The Games I Played

The above are just a few examples. Material things were more important to me than sex. Because I could get sex on the regular, my objective was to try to get ahead financially. Tearing down a woman's self-esteem was so easy to do. I wasn't considering that the things I was doing would come back on me, nor that I may have scared these women into not trusting the next man who may come along and want more for her than I did. I was not very thoughtful when it came to that. I started thinking about my worth as a man. That consisted of:

- **What was my gift to women?**
- **How could I be a great man and find that special woman?**

I had no clue. I started thinking that I did not deserve to be with a woman. I believed my gift was to ruin every woman I met. I was pretending to be this Prince Charming only to turn out to be a villain to women. They say physically abusing a woman is the worst thing one can do to lower her self-esteem. That may be true but verbally and mentally abusing them seemed to be far more effective.

Derrick Taylor

There is a saying that women are put on this earth to make men better. If that's true, I took that statement literally because if she wasn't helping me to enhance myself I had no use for her. I didn't care about her well-being. My attitude was that I could get any woman I wanted, and I did not care how I went about doing it. If that were my goal, that was the goal I would meet. I thought women were as scandalous as men, and if that were the case I was not going to be played by any of them. My ultimate goals were to play women and be very sneaky about it before they got the chance to do it to me. It never occurred to me that not all women were the same. Most women want to be loved and most women want that honest, strong, and reliable man for security.

My attitude did not allow me to think that way. The fact was that I did not trust women and I used them for everything they had. My friends that were in relationships, used to tell me that I may find myself alone if I did not change my approach toward women. That thought may have been true but I wanted to play the game to the fullest.

MORAL

In this chapter, I admit that I used to take advantage of women for sex and material possessions. Today I have noticed that some women give up sex too easy. Women need to know that if they do give up sex as soon as they meet a man, he may not respect you and that may not make him want to be with you for the right reasons. It is one thing to support a man, but taking care of him is another. If a man can work and provide for himself, let him do just that. We as men need and should want women in our lives, so ladies know your worth and your value.

Man Up!

Product of My Environment

Chapter 3

Product of My Environment

> *Many families endure pain, suffering, and plenty of ups and downs. My life may not be different from many others, but my familial background played a significant role in shaping who I am today. I share with you the trials and tribulations I encountered in my family life. I truly do not believe that a person should remain the same individual later in life that they were growing up, despite whatever hardship they come from. Anyone and everyone can change.*
>
> ~D. Taylor

3

Product of My Environment

I became such a disrespectful person as a result of the lack of focus I had as a child. I do believe people can change despite whatever environment they may come from. I never took up the personal responsibility to improve myself. I never took the time to realize that how I grew up did not have to make me who I had become.

When I was born into this world my mother was only 23 and already had three children prior to me, one girl and two boys. Two years later she had my younger brother with a different man, not my father. This would be the kind of lifestyle that I would grow up in as a child trying to understand the reality of my siblings, and I having different fathers. We were still very close and enjoyed each other despite those circumstances. Every day seemed to be a challenge, but a hurdle we would overcome. This included the difficulties I experienced as a child.

As a child, I had a heart murmur causing me to be in and out of the hospital on a weekly basis. Due to complications I had to have a tube inserted into my chest to monitor the strength of my heart. I was a very hyper kid and my heart wasn't strong enough to endure that hyperactivity. I was often unable to be active the way my siblings could. At times, my mother would have to hold me in her arms just so I could not run and play like the other kids.

> **Heart murmurs or congenital heart defects are the most common cause of abnormal heart murmurs in children. These defects are problems with the hearts structure that are present at birth. They change the normal flow of blood to the heart. Some babies are born with more than one heart defect.**

When I think about those stories my mother used to tell me as I became older, I realized how that played a big role in how I behaved as an adult. I became very spoiled because of the treatment I was receiving from my mother and

Product of My Environment

the rest of the family. I received different punishments than my siblings. I could essentially get anything I wanted if I just said that my heart was bothering me. Not only was that wrong of me, but also it was crippling me as I grew into a man.

As a kid I remember certain things about our living conditions. We did not have much to brag about, my mother was a single parent and did everything she could to make our living arrangements better. The dreams of her going to college were shortened because her focus was making sure she was there for her kids. She was working jobs making very little money, certainly not enough to support the family, but doing the best that she could. One of her jobs was working in a nursing home helping elderly patients. During these years, the 80s' to be exact, the pay rate was around $4.15, so she had to work many long hours to make a descent paycheck. I remember waking up to get dropped off at my grandmother's house most mornings when my mom had to go to work. Although we did have a place to stay, most of our time was spent with our grandmother.

Derrick Taylor

*****

Derrick's Truth: At one point we lived in a two-bedroom apartment in which one-bedroom was shared by me and my siblings. At times we did not have all the necessities that one should have. We had to live in conditions such as not having water, lights, and heat because of not having the money to pay the bills. These problems did not occur all at one time, of course.

*****

My mom was a popular statistic growing up. She was a teenage mother and financially she would at times struggle to make ends meet. She longed for a personal life and dated men looking for a relationship for herself and a provider for us. I would compare my mom to a young mother in the twenty-first century-one who is in her teens when she has her baby out of wedlock and looks for help from her mother to help raise the child. Because of my mother's situation, we would sometimes go to live with my grandmother for a while. It became a comfortable setting for us. After staying with our grandmother for quite some time, we would start calling her "mama" and referring to our biological mom by her first name. We knew she was our mom, but we did not call her that.

Sometimes, I believed that we were not family-oriented. The conditions I grew up in may not have been that different from other families because there are ups and downs in all phases of life-but it seemed from my point of view that all we encountered were the down times. To me, everything my family tried to accomplish often times faded from existence. Today when I think about it, I feel bad about what my mom went through. It became so hard for her to enjoy her life because she'd had kids at such a young age. She never had the time to enjoy the luxury of living the lifestyle any woman in her twenties would want to live, but I am happy to say that I would not trade my mom for any other mother in the world.

Despite the circumstances, we remained her top priority and the little money she did make she did the very best trying to provide for us and while at the same time trying to enjoy herself. Just as teen parents do, she relied on her mother (my grandmother) to take care of us when she wanted to go out. My mom never had much help from our fathers. The little help she did get went to us and bills. We hardly ever lived in a stable environment if we weren't in our grandmother's home. We constantly moved around because we could not maintain our living expenses due to financial hardships. Sometimes we would live with different relatives, which at times separated us. It wasn't that often because my siblings and I did not get along with most of them. Another reason we did not stay with our family members other than our grandmother was due to promises made and broken by my mom. She would sometimes tell them that she would pay them to keep us but did not when it came time to pay up.

- **I guess that's a flaw I inherited from my mother, which was not paying my bills on time.**
- **I'm like my mom because I had a hard time getting along with the people around me as I got older.**

Product of My Environment

The good thing about moving around so much was that we could make plenty of new friends. I never had the luxury of having many decent clothes or nice shoes.

Because of our misfortunes, I used to borrow my brothers clothes. Due to our living arrangements, my mom had to apply for welfare, which did help some. A few times she had to exchange food stamps for cash to make bill payments. Most kids would be ashamed that their family had to resort to welfare but I didn't look at it that way because it allowed us to have food and live somewhat stable. As a child, I did not know much but what I did know was that our lifestyle was not that lavish and we just had to learn to adjust. We had to make the best of what we had. We did not have the answers all the time, but one thing my brothers and I did have was street smarts.

> **What we took from our mom was to always be strong and whatever you decide to do be the very best that you can be. And most important is to never give up no matter how hard life gets.**

Derrick Taylor

In order for us to get what we wanted, we started finding ways to make money. Between ages that ranged from nine to 13, we would collect Coca-Cola bottles worth 10 cents each; we would cut the grass, wash cars, whatever we could to make a little change. I remember my uncles and aunts giving us money to go play their daily numbers, and I would make at least 50 cents doing that. Just as they have the lottery today, we had local gambling in our neighborhood. Running numbers was illegal, but we didn't know too much about that. No one was going to give us anything, so the only thing we knew how to do at such a young age was hustle. *If we did not try to make it on our own, we knew that we would not get much help from anyone else*.

We knew the struggles we had; after living in many neighborhoods, our mindset was to try to make our lives easier, and help our mother as much as possible. Our goal was to help my mother upgrade to a better place other than that small two-bedroom apartment we had. Sharing a bed with my siblings was not very comfortable, not to mention that my seven-year-old brother Tony was a bed-wetter. Not only were we dealing with that issue, but also the apartment was not very clean, we also had a problem with pests and rodents. We had to make the best out of what we could afford because my mom, working as a certified nursing assistant part-time, was making only 800 dollars a month for six people, and we were living on welfare which did not give us much. Our Biggest problem was food. With growing boys in the house having enough food in the house seemed to be a constant problem. I recall being made fun of by some of my so-called friends. They would make comments like, "the poor family." They would pick at my clothes because at times I would have to wear the same thing repeatedly. Although I did have friends who would help some of the time I mostly kept to myself. After several months in our apartment, we began to encounter even more problems. When it would rain, floodwaters would run into our apartment. After experiencing several floods, we adapted to the idea that when it rained it could very well flood our apartment.

*****

Derrick's Truth: One afternoon a huge storm passed through my hometown, Statesboro. It rained all day and into the night. As the rain got heavier and heavier the water began to seep into our apartment, rising higher and higher. We soon realized that everything in the apartment was going to be destroyed, not to mention that myself and my three brothers were in the apartment. Luckily my sister wasn't there at the time. The worst thing about our apartment was its location. Being that it was near a wooded area we would sometimes see snakes. All of this came into consideration when our home flooded. Luckily, some friends in the neighborhood remembering my mother with four little boys came to our rescue. One by one, we jumped on their backs and they carried us through the waters to safety.

*****

Due to this misfortune, we had to stay with our grandmother and try to figure out what our next move would be. When that flood hit, we lost the few possessions we had. What little clothes and shoes we had were gone. All we had were the clothes on our backs. What a disaster. We faced one setback after another, but we had to keep our composure.

Product of My Environment

I remember jumping for joy when my mom was finally able to get her first home. Working hard and long hours and saving her money was the reason she could afford the home (it was a white wooden house with three-bedrooms and two-bathrooms). Having more space to move around, we enjoyed living life the way it should be. Although we did not have much furniture at the time, she did the best that she could. At least we had a home, well at least for a little while we did. One night something drastic happened. I awoke to my mom screaming for us to get up and get out of the house. I got up and saw smoke everywhere. Our brand new house had caught on fire. Once again, our lives were at a turning point. Everything had burned in the fire and our house was gone. It's amazing how much one family can go through in such a short time. I thought that we were the only family having hard times and I decided that I just did not care. That was the attitude I adopted as I got older. I lost trust in everything and blamed my family's misfortune on everyone. I developed a negative spirit that stayed with me as I matured.

Derrick Taylor

With all of the problems we were constantly facing it become exhausting. I did not want to move anymore, I just wanted to be stable and have a solid, reliable home. As she began to cry more often, I could sense my mother throwing in the towel. She had nowhere else to turn, and she could not get the help she needed. Sometimes she would leave for days, trying to find a solution. We did not understand it at the time but we knew she wasn't herself anymore. We started to think that we were in the way of her achieving a better life which she so desperately wanted. The misfortunes my mom had kept us from having the life that most young children dream of having. We hardly spent holidays together as a family; we hardly enjoyed Christmas and Thanksgiving as a family. When our birthdays came around, we did not have birthday parties. Our goal was to just make it the best way we knew how.

> I'm by no means judging my mom but as a kid witnessing those things you get a confusing example and become angry that things are going so badly for your family, and majority of the time you end up blaming the head of household.

MORAL

In this chapter I admit that we had many struggles to overcome, but as a family we remained close. How this played a part in my life in mistreating women was that growing up without much led me to use women to get what I needed. No man should use how he grew up as an excuse to get over on people. Always remember that whatever struggles you encountered as a child you can overcome them.

Man Up!

My Youth Development

Chapter 4

My Youth Development

> *Kids are a product of their environment. But despite any obstacles your child might face, always try to be in their life and raise them to be a good person. Times do get tough, but never give up on your child. Always believe that they can make a difference.*
>
> ~D. Taylor

4

My Youth Development

Growing up my siblings and I tried to become closer as a family and started hanging out with one another more frequently. My grandmother's house was convenient to the other children in the neighborhood, so we embraced it. We started meeting other kids some were fun to be around, and others were a bad influence but because of what we had been through, we were accustomed to the bad and tough behavior of other children.

It did not get any better once we started to develop and hang out with the other children in the neighborhood. We were different ages and I saw my siblings starting to hang out with their respective age groups, a development

I disapprove of because I wanted us to stay close to each other. I didn't understand that we could go in different directions, but remain close as a family. I was afraid to hang out with other children in the neighborhood because I was shy and spoiled and wanted everything to go my way, so I never learned how to make friends without my brothers around me. I started hanging out by myself and became very antisocial. I started acting out toward my brothers and wanted to be by myself all the time.

Everyone noticed the change in my behavior and did not approve of it. No one had any idea what was wrong with me. I became this hyper child with a lot of energy. I became so out of control and poorly behaved to the point that no one wanted to have anything to do with me. The reason being:

My Youth Development

- **I was a terrible kid who enjoyed seeing another person injured or in pain.**
- **I would go places I knew I had no business going, just so that people would worry about me.**
- **I knew I would get away with my behavior because I had an excuse—my heart condition.**
- **If I was punished for anything, all I had to do was say that my heart was bothering me.**

I was screaming for attention. When I knew I was going to get a whipping, I would immediately yell, "My heart hurts!" I knew I could get away with it because I had a heart murmur. My siblings would see that and get mad at me, and distance themselves from me. Noticing that, I became even more disobedient to everyone. No one knew me better than my oldest brother, Michael. Although he would not let me hang with him, he did his best to challenge me to become a better person. Unfortunately, challenging me did not change my behavior it only made it worse. Anything Michael told me would go in one ear and out the other, rendering it useless. I couldn't be helped; at least not by my

Derrick Taylor

family. We weren't the type of family who would sit down together and talk through our problems. They were always solved outside of the home. My problems grew worse when I would be hanging out in our neighborhood. Everything I learned, I learned hanging out in the streets. The more I got to know our neighborhood, the more trouble I got into.

*****

Derrick's Truth: I remember going to a grocery store called Piggly Wiggly, to steal candy. With no reason behind it I just did it for fun. I wore this big green jacket with fur around the hood, as if it were below-zero outside, but it was summertime. I would walk into the store and proceed to the candy aisle, grabbing a handful of family-sized packs of Snickers bars and Butterfingers. After I loaded up my jacket, I would leave the store as if no one saw me. Stealing was not helping my character but what I wanted I would do everything in my power to get.

*****

Another new challenge for me was entering the first grade. Right away I decided that I had to become the center

My Youth Development

of attention at school. I became angry with teachers and students for no reason. I picked on girls because I knew I could dominate them. I had to make numerous trips to the principal's office. I just became a terrible child. I could not make friends at the school. I had gotten this reputation as a bully and no one wanted to be around me. When my class took field trips, I could never go because I was always in trouble. However, there was one trip that I did take often during my school year.

I remember a White man in a red truck coming to get me from school and taking me to this big office building miles away from my school. Placed in a room all by myself with lots of toys and games, I would have so much fun, realizing that I was the only one playing in this room every day. I did not know why this man was so nice, but I became accustomed to him giving me practically anything I asked for because I was leaving with this man every day. I assumed everybody hated me or they didn't want me in school, I had no idea. The next thing I realized was that this man was giving me pills to take when I was with him. They were these small white pills that tasted sweet, so I thought they were some kind of mint or some kind of candy I was receiving as a reward. I started asking my mother questions about this man I was leaving school with and what were these pills he was giving me. I learned three things:

> - **The man I was leaving with every day was a psychiatric doctor.**
> - **The pills I thought were candy turned out to be Ritalin, which subdued my hyperactivity and energetic, disordered behavior.**
> - **I was diagnosed with Attention Deficit Disorder.**

__Fact:__ It is estimated that between 3-5% of preschool and school-age children have ADHD or approximately 2 million children in the United States. That means in a class of 25 to 30 students, it is likely that at least one student will have this common condition. Studies estimate that 30-70% of children with ADHD will continue to have symptom into adolescent and adulthood.

My A.D.D was so out of control that I would do bad things to people like throw rocks at then, hit them, and push

My Youth Development

them off the swing. Most of the time I would not remember what happened when it was brought to my attention. I was never disciplined for the things I did; I was only confronted. When I arrived back at school, I noticed I was placed into classes with other kids who behaved like me. I now thought, "I finally have friends I can relate to, kids who share the same passion as me." I started noticing things and began to pay attention to certain details. I was not with the children from my neighborhood. I would see them going to lunch as I would be leaving lunch, and I started to understand that my classroom was in a trailer away from the school and I wondered what the difference was. The difference was that they were in regular classes and I was in special classes with kids who needed special attention. I realized if I were going to be reunited with my peers, I would have to get my act together. I couldn't function and pay attention long enough to help myself achieve better grades. Consequently, I ended up repeating the first grade.

Later, in my adolescent years, I began to focus more on my schoolwork and excelling in the classroom. The reason was because my past and my reputation as a disrespectful child meant that I did not have many friends, enabling me to focus more on my work. I remember being in a fifth grade average class that guaranteed I would be with some of my friends from my neighborhood. I thought that was where I needed to be (during my elementary school days our school system separated students based on grade levels; above-average students were on A-level status, and average students were on B-level status), the challenge was beneath me. I excelled far more than my friends and was given a more challenging offer. Later in the year I was moved to the above-average class where I was united with a predominantly White peer group. That was something new considering where I grew up. My friends started to see that I had left their classroom and they started to distance themselves from me, calling me names and telling me that I thought I was better than them. After all that I became rebellious and did not want to be in accelerated classes. So I started letting my grades slip just so I could fail and prove to my friends that I was still like them. I just wanted to be accepted and did not realize what was best for my future. My schoolwork became a distant second to my friends. No matter how hard

My Youth Development

I tried to fit in, I realized that I was not going to satisfy everybody. I had become a joke.

Once known as a bully and earning a bad reputation, I was now the boy who became the victim. Because my family did not have much money that meant that I couldn't get many clothes, shoes, or anything that most families would pick up from the mall. My friends started to notice, and that's when the torture began. I knew I had to fend for myself, so my attitude became selfish. I stopped caring about anything. I started picking fights and no one wanted to be around me. Although I was bad as hell, I started focusing on my class work so that I could advance to the next grade level in hopes of leaving my friends behind. At 13 and in the sixth grade, the school introduced sports programs that I could join. I remembered how gifted my brothers and I used to be with sports when we were little, and I knew I had to try to excel at sports again. My oldest brother Michael, who is three years older than me and in high school, excelled in basketball. So I started distancing myself from my friends who teased me, and I started hanging with Michael more. I could see the change in him and how much people wanted to be around him and I wanted to be my brother. Before this change in my life, there was a drastic change for my younger brother Tony.

The summer before my sixth-grade year, my two older brothers and my sister were hardly around, I was left to look after Tony. I remember one afternoon I had a fever that was so high that I could not bear to get out of bed. I heard this loud screaming and the front door burst open, making me leap out of bed. I proceeded to close my door, thinking it was the neighborhood dogs that got loose and chased my brother in the house (there were some huge dogs in our neighborhood who would run free sometimes), but it wasn't the dogs, I soon realized it was the sound of my mother screaming and my younger brother shouting, "I can't see, I can't see!" Tony had been the victim of a gunshot to the eye, leaving him blind in his left eye. I can still so clearly remember seeing all that blood in the house and on his shirt. My mother was terrified; she picked up the phone and dialed 911 immediately. She was trying to wait on the ambulance to come but the wait was too long for her so we loaded in the car and took Tony to the hospital. After surgery and the at-

My Youth Development

tempt to save his eye Tony was left with the sight of just one eye. I was so upset that my fever was no longer a factor, and all I could think about was getting revenge on whoever did this to Tony. That never happened because I never got a chance to find the boy who had done it.

After that accident, I felt as if I had failed to protect my little brother. I started thinking I was neither dependable nor reliable, and those characteristics seemed to stick as a label throughout my adolescent and teenage years. When I was 13 we were off and moving again. This time the country side of town was more suitable for my mother. Again I made more new friends, but this time it was a little different. These friends were more into girls, and at that point in my life I had never even kissed a girl, much less what these guys were doing to girls. It was then that I met Sam who had a reputation of being good with and was actually having sex with girls (Sam was at least two years older than me).

*****

Derrick's Truth: One day we were hanging out at his house when we heard a girl he knew calling for him from next door. I guess that was some kind of hint that she was home by herself because we proceeded to head next door. As we entered her house, she was standing there naked; I was amazed and my hormones were raging. I did not know what it was at the time, but whatever it was it I had a good feeling. Sam laid down with this girl and all I could hear was the sound of two bodies colliding and the sound of the girl's voice, as if she were in pain. As her noises subsided and I could no longer hear their bodies coming together, I heard my name called to come into the room. I went in, and the girl was lying on the ground, still naked, and Sam told me that she wanted me and that I should take off my clothes. Without hesitation I did just that. He handed me a condom, which I knew nothing about, and I put it on and began having sex with this girl. I had no idea what I was doing, but I knew it felt good to do it. Then a weird thing started to happen. I noticed a feeling funny, as if I were wetting the bed, so I jumped up and looked at my friend and said, "What is that?" Sam looked at me and laughing, said, "You had an orgasm and you're a man now." Realizing I was not a virgin anymore I went hopping and skipping

My Youth Development

home because I had just lost my virginity at the age of 13. My life with girls would never be the same after that.

*****

Now in a new location, I still had problems getting along with other kids. I made some friends; I lost some friends. The friends I lost became my enemies. Fight after fight, things did not get any better. The difference this time was that Michael became a significant part of my life, trying to teach me right from wrong. The more he tried, the more it went through one ear and straight out the other. I remember Michael telling me the only way to fend for myself was to get involved with sports as he did. I knew I had the skills, but I did not apply myself enough. I wasn't motivated. It was not until I had seen Michael perform in a game that I became interested in pursuing sports. I saw how he and his friends would act around each other, as if they were brothers. So I began to want that. After playing football and basketball for a while, I started to gain that brotherhood. The difference was that I used that popularity to control the people around me because I knew I was the shit. That was the beginning of another trait that would follow me into my adult years. The more popular I became in sports, the more a crowd grew of girls. My relationship with girls became so easy that I could get the attention of any girl in school I wanted at least that's what I thought at the time. It turned out it was only because I was this great athlete that everyone wanted to be around during those respective seasons; I could not have felt any more used than that.

As my relationship with sports grew stronger, my dedication to my schoolwork faded. I ended up flunking the seventh grade because of my poor decisions. I never took anything seriously except for my relationship with sports. To get myself back on track I enrolled in summer school, but that turned out to be a bad investment because the only thing I did was drop out. I thought I was too good for summer school. I had also become a quitter, another trait that would follow me into my adult years. The school year began with me restarting the seventh grade. I was so embarrassed that I wanted to drop out of school. I thought there was no reason to even be there. So I became determined and tried hard to succeed that year. I told myself that I was not going to give up again. I had become a joke to so many people. It had gotten to the point where I was just talk and no action. No one pays attention to a failure that makes false promises. I became a distraction to the people around me who took their schoolwork seriously. I had to do something to regain the trust of my peers. Because I only cared about sports, and I was perceived as being dumb, no one had any faith in me anymore. I couldn't play sports if I did not have the grades. I applied myself and began to do what was necessary to pass the seventh grade. The end of the school year arrived and all my friends were going to high school, but I was entering the eighth grade, or so I thought. When I received my report card, I saw that I would be advancing to the ninth grade with the rest of my class. The reason behind them skipping me was because the school board implemented an age limit that a student should be in middle school and I was past that age limit. I was ecstatic. I was going to be in high school with my two older brothers, Michael, James, and my friends from middle school. What a blessing that was.

Derrick Taylor

Now in high school and reunited with my friends, I became calmer, but seemed to be more of an arrogant person in the eyes of many of my friends. I got ahead of myself, but some of my friends still thought of me as a joke. They would say things like; I did not have an eighth-grade education and that I skipped a grade because I was too old and not because of my hard work. Sometimes I felt bad about the things they were saying, but I knew what a better situation I was in at that point. After a little self-motivation and gaining my confidence back, I wanted to be around people whom were thinking about and pursuing college, and people who had an idea of what they wanted to do with their lives. Those goals and having my older brother Michael around to guide me would help me succeed; at least that's what I thought. I could begin to see a pattern in my behavior. This time not only were sports a big part of my life but also in high school my focus was directed toward girls. It did not help that I was the younger brother of a star basketball player which got me the attention I was seeking. I would feed off my brother's accomplishments and used those to my advantage. Not only was that not the right thing

My Youth Development

to do, but as it turns out it would cripple me in years to come.

MORAL+

In this chapter I took many things for granted; my schoolwork, and the ability to be an outstanding student. This played a significant role in my adult life because when I got older I did not take things seriously. Whatever I did I did not give it my all; whether it was the relationships I was in or the jobs that I had, I wasn't dependable. Whatever you choose to do in life, give it your all. Never take anything for granted and never let your past failures dictate your future.

Man Up!

Short of My Expectations

Chapter 5

Short of My Expectations

> *Life can be difficult. People are always looking for an influence—someone to look up to, someone to emulate. You can set the example; be the person that people want to be like. You can help change the world by changing yourself.*
>
> ~D. Taylor

5

Short of My Expectations

*****

Derrick's Truth: In 1993 and 1994 I excelled in basketball. I was six feet, four inches tall, about 185 pounds and could play any guard positions on the basketball court extremely well. I had been recruited by several Division One college basketball teams. I was one of the top basketball players in the state of Georgia. I was selected All-State and I received *Street and Smith's* All-American, All-Region honors, and I was nominated to the 1994 McDonald's All-American Team.

*****

Derrick Taylor

I always wanted to be like my brother Michael. He received the attention of so many basketball scouts in high school. At 16 years of age I thought that was the coolest thing on the planet and something I wanted to emulate. I started stealing his clothes to wear to school in order to portray his image, so that I could be at least half the person he was. It did not benefit me to immolate Michael as much as I did. At the time, yes, but in later years, I let myself get out of control.

In August of 1991, Michael was off to Auburn University on a basketball scholarship. During his senior year, his team won the state high school basketball championship. I worked extremely hard that year after he left, thinking only of my brother's accomplishments. My ninth-grade year turned out to be great. After my brother left, I lost my sense of focus and started hanging around the wrong crowds. Not only that, the selfishness I had exhibited when I was in the seventh grade started to resurface. The attention my brother was giving me I wasn't getting, and because of those issues my grades declined.

Short of My Expectations

I was becoming a failure again. My focus reverted back to primarily sports and girls instead of my grades. I was unable to maintain my grades the first semester of my tenth grade year. The worst thing that could happen to a student athlete happened to me which was getting kicked off my high school basketball team. Once I lost the privilege to play basketball, I gave up. At the young age of 17, I went from bad to worse almost overnight. I started drinking, skipping school, and I even started smoking marijuana with some distant friends. The student athletes I used to hang with viewed me differently. That brotherhood saw me as a total loser. I would drown my self-pity in my drinking. I was giving up everything I had worked hard to get. I just did not have the drive I once had, becoming a nobody. I was on the path to jail or death. Michael heard about my behavior. He reached out to me, but my bothers words went in one ear and out the other. Once again my life was headed in the wrong direction, I had to either make it or be nothing at all.

*****

Derrick Taylor

Derrick's Truth: One Saturday night my drinking habits had increased severely to the point where I just had to have it on a regular basis. My friends Sam and Richard and I decided to go buy some alcohol and pick up some marijuana so we could have a good time. After we'd gotten everything we headed back to the house, drinking, and smoking all night. We were drunk and high, and we decided to head to the Georgia Southern University campus in Statesboro to see some college girls we'd met. As we got to the parking lot, campus security pulled us over because we had a tail light out. We did our best to hide our weed and alcohol. My heart was pounding out of my chest, and the sweat was dripping from my body. The security officer asked us to get out of the car. They noticed the smell of beer on our breath and in the car. The officer asked if we had been drinking, and as scared as I was, I answered, "Yes sir, officer, we were drinking." We had to take a Breathalyzer test, which revealed that we were over the legal limit. We were arrested and charged with minor possession of alcohol, a sentence that carried one year of probation under our parents' supervision. After being detained, we had our photos taken,

Short of My Expectations

were released to our parents, and suffered the embarrassment of having our names printed in the local newspaper.

*****

What a major blow to my reputation, it was sincerely humiliating. All my potential was now viewed as a waste of talent to those in my hometown. My determination was to turn myself around after that incident. I vowed to take advantage of any opportunity that would come my way. In 1993, my situation got a little better. My skills as an outstanding basketball player emerged as I was named to the region's all-tournament team. Our basketball team was one of the best teams in the state of Georgia. Not only was my junior season a great year but also my senior season, which I received all state honors and was nominated to the McDonald's All-American team. Despite my many struggles I graduated from Statesboro High School in 1994. My goal was to get a division one scholarship, but because I did not get a qualifying score on my SAT, I received an athletic scholarship to play basketball at LB Wallace Community College in Andalusia, Alabama. I thought I was on my way to a better life. This was the most I had ever accomplished and I thought I was going to be alright.

After receiving the scholarship, the only thing I had to do was get to college, do what it took to succeed, and graduate. None of that happened; that part of my life became a wasted opportunity. The reason being was because I still had that selfish arrogant attitude that I deserved better and that a community college was beneath me. I did not take it seriously. Instead of having a positive attitude and being grateful of the situation, I gave up. After just one semester I quit and no longer wanted any part of that institution. I played a total of 13 games for the basketball team. Being at this community college located in a small town, I perceived myself as being better than the basketball players I was playing against. It wasn't a challenge to me. I left college, moved back home to Statesboro to live with my mother, and got a job at a Shoney's restaurant, where I washed dishes and was a short-order cook. So I was this college dropout with no experience, working in a restaurant as a cook.

Short of My Expectations

The most embarrassing thing was seeing the classmates and teachers who once believed in my potential look down on me for giving up on a good education and an amazing opportunity to play college basketball, the sport I loved so much. I felt belittled working in this restaurant, trying to hide everything. Dropping out of college and not having any goals, I had to figure out how to make my life better. I wasn't thinking of going back to college, but rather how I could make some fast money. I ended up turning to friends who I knew were doing the wrong things to make money, they were selling drugs. I was curious about how to sell drugs myself, but because I did not know too much about that business, my friends gave me the job of a drug runner. A runner was the person who would take a large amount of drugs to a specific location, unlike a dealer standing on the corner to sell his goods.

After running drugs for a year, I realized that I could be missing any chance I had left to correct my life, and I knew I needed to get out of the drug game. It was not until I got stopped by a police officer on my way to make a drop-off that I followed through with that promise. That moment, I knew God was with me; when the police stopped me I had drugs with me not to mention I had been drinking and smoking with my friends earlier that day. The only thing the police asked for was my identification. I was scared as hell while praying silently. They stopped me for questioning to see if I was a part of a group of boys who stole from a store that was in the area. They ended up searching me but did not find anything and let me go. Since God got me off the hook, I knew at that moment I would never deal with drugs again.

After giving the drug game up that year, I enrolled at East Georgia College for a semester. Then I enrolled at Middle Georgia College for a year of studies to get myself back on track. Again, I fell short. Despite everything I had been through, I quit college just as I did before. I was academically suspended. I had no focus and no drive. I found myself back at home again, doing absolutely nothing. I had no responsibilities, I had no life, and all of my friends were nowhere to be found.

Short of My Expectations

> - **I had no goals because I was only concerned about living in the moment.**
> - **No plans because I didn't vision myself being a productive citizen.**
> - **And no motivation because I didn't have that motivator to push me.**

At this point, I had no choice but to get a job and try to do something with my life because I feared that running drugs would land me in jail as it did most of my friends and I wanted no part of that. I ended up working in a siding warehouse loading trucks making 10 dollars an hour. I had bad habit of blowing the money that I did make. I was very flamboyant and always living above my means. ***This was a bad habit to have and one that I would carry into adulthood.***

After working this job for at least a year, and when I turned 21, I convinced my sister to co-sign with me for my first car and the reason for her to co-sign was that my credit was not good enough to get it on my own. She agreed, and I wish now she had not because I ended up making her credit go bad. The car was a blue two-door 1995 Chevy Cavalier Coupe. I fell so in love with that car that the only thing I forgot to do was make the payments on the car. What an irresponsible thing to do because I splurged a lot, and I wasted my money on hanging out with my friends instead of making my payments. My mindset was if I made the payments I wouldn't have money to hang out. After four months or so of making no payments, I got a phone call from my sister accusing me of not paying the car notes. I insisted that I had, but I was lying (lying became a big part of my life). After denying that I was not making payments on the car, it got repossessed.

Everything about me had become a lie. I would lie about the littlest things just to get ahead. It got to the point where I would lie to my mother and tell her that I still had a job when I didn't. I had lost my job because I was constantly late to work. Eventually she got fed up with my behavior and kicked me out of the house. I had nowhere to go and when I refused to leave, she did the only thing I thought she would never do, she called the police on me. The worst was yet to come. I ended up staying with my friends who I was

Short of My Expectations

running drugs for. It got so bad that my friends did not want me around because I didn't want to run drugs for them any longer. After that I had nowhere to turn. I remember crying because I could not depend on anybody. I lost faith in myself and didn't care what happened to me. The one person I did believe in was Michael, and he was hundreds of miles away in Baton Rouge, Louisiana. I figured that was my only option to turn my life around, so I picked up a pay phone, calling him collect, and begging him to come get me. After talking for several minutes, he agreed. The next day he drove down to pick me up and on June 1, 1998 I was living in with my brother in Baton Rouge, Louisiana.

MORAL

In this chapter I discussed all the opportunities I had, but did not take advantage of. Creating an image for one's self is important if it's a positive image. I did not stay true to myself and had to go through a difficult period before things got better. Always remember that a good perception can take an individual far in life. Avoid falling short of personal goals which can only hinder your success in life. Try to create a positive image and become someone people can depend on. Everyone has one life to live so try to make the best of it.

Man Up!

A Walk in My Shoes

Chapter 6

A Walk in My Shoes

This is an example of how so many of us are still working things out on some level, though some of us dare not admit it. Become your own person and believe in yourself, because if you don't, no one else will.

~D. Taylor

6

A Walk in My Shoes

My life in Louisiana seemed to be exactly what I needed. I was 23 beginning a new phase in my life and starting fresh. I was going to do what was necessary to become a better person. Just like when we were younger, Michael was something of a father figure to me. I always wanted to be like him and obtain his accomplishments. He always stayed on me to do the right things, and I would listen to him, but just could not do what he said. So the saga continued.

I was in a different state with different surroundings. The person I truly was would not be recognizable in these new surroundings. I could easily start fresh and project the image of a respectable person who came from a great background and I knew I wouldn't be known as a liar or a manipulator. I had no intention of changing who I was. My brother laid down several rules, the rules were as follows:

> - **I had to get a job so that I could save money and get my own place.**
> - **Help out with the bills that would be created by me living there.**
> - **Change my ways and become better than I used to be.**

I did not do any of that. After working six months at Wal-Mart I lost the job because I was never on time. I did not help out with bills much because I would spend my money as soon as I got paid, and because of that I could not save any money. I was doing the same thing I was doing back home in Statesboro, Georgia, only I was doing it in Baton Rouge, Louisiana.

I did meet and date people there, but again it was only for pleasure, nothing serious. I knew once I got to Baton Rouge that I was not going to live here because I didn't like it and I was homesick. After about eight months I met a

A Walk in My Shoes

beautiful light-skinned woman named June. From the moment I met June I fell for her, but I lied to her about everything. When she asked me where I was from instead of mentioning my hometown, I named the most popular city close by which was Atlanta. I thought that would give me more credibility, and she wouldn't think I was a country boy. When she asked me what college I attended I would tell her Georgia Southern University. I thought I would be seen as being smarter rather than say I went to a community college. Any question she asked me, I responded with lie after lie. The more we hung out, the more lies I told. After about three months dating June, she ended the "relationship" because she found the truth behind many lies that I was telling her. It did not stop me from pursuing other girls.

My stay in Louisiana was only a year and I hadn't accomplished anything. My ways still hadn't changed. Finally, my brother was getting tired of my shit and decided it was time to be on my own. I knew he was serious this time because he had landed a job in Atlanta and had begun to pack up his apartment leaving me to figure it out on my own. I had no option but to go back home, which I knew would be a disaster. I had no money saved up and had only a month to work out a solution before he had to leave.

Prior to losing my job at Wal-Mart, I did fill out applications at several companies. One in particular was Heilig Meyers Furniture for a Sales Associate position. I remember getting the call for an interview. I borrowed some slacks and a tie from my brother and headed to the interview. When I arrived there was a long line of applicants, I assumed mostly college students because they looked very young. Each of the applicants had résumés and if they were college students I assumed they had college experience. I had none of those things, but I also had no other choice. I did not want to go back to Statesboro so I had to gain my composure and get in line. The line got shorter and shorter, and finally it was my turn to be interviewed.

I went into the office and there were two White men sitting at a table. I was so nervous I was sweating bullets. They asked me for my résumé; I didn't have one. They asked me for references; I had none. I was asked if I had any prior skills at being a Sales Associate and I told them that I had never done that type of work. They smiled and

A Walk in My Shoes

threw me a pen and asked me to sell it to them. I described the color, the shape, and the benefits that they could receive from that pen. I just had that niche about making something believable. I made that pen seem as if that were the only pen to have. They were shocked and very impressed. They thanked me and said that they would get in touch with me if they needed me. The only things that would have kept me from getting that job were my lack of education and experience because I was that confident.

After the interview it took me about 30 minutes to get home. Once I got home I saw my brother, and immediately started packing my things. I was devastated. It felt as if I were being kicked out of college and forced to leave the premises. I had to call my mother to ask if I could come home, something I definitely did not want to do. When I got to the phone to make that call, I noticed the message light blinking on the phone and I checked the message. Surprisingly, it was the furniture company calling to tell me that I got the job, what a relief. After two weeks of working there it was time for my brother to move to Atlanta, and I had to find a way to transfer my job. As of June 1999, I had been in Louisiana for only a year, and. my brother was already packed and ready to move to Atlanta. I had been with the company for only two weeks, so in order to make this happen I had to come up with a convincing story. I did what I do best, I lied. I told them that my stepfather had colon cancer and I needed to go back home to help take care of him. I knew right then I could lie about anything as long as it benefited me. The lie was so convincing that I was transferred to another Heilig Meyers Furniture store in Atlanta, Georgia.

MORAL

In this chapter I mention having many second chances to do the right thing but I did not take advantage of those chances. Opportunities may knock at your door and then again they may not. If provided another opportunity utilize it because that may be the only chance you get.

Man Up!

My Lack of Ambition

Chapter 7

My Lack of Ambition

> *Many people have never stopped to consider these questions. What is the meaning of life? How can purpose, fulfillment, and satisfaction be found? How can something of lasting significance be achieved? So many people have never stopped to consider these important questions. They look back years later and wonder why their relationships have fallen apart and why they feel so empty, even though they may have achieved what they set out to accomplish. People pursue many things, thinking that in them they will find meaning. Some of these pursuits include business success, wealth, good relationships, sex, entertainment, and doing good deeds. People have testified that while they achieved their goals of wealth, relationships, and pleasure, they were still left with a deep void inside; a feeling of emptiness that nothing seemed to fill.*
>
> *~D. Taylor*

7

My Lack of Ambition

Now at 24, my responsibilities began to take a backseat when it came to my social life. I was in Atlanta, a city much larger than Baton Rouge with much more to do; more clubs, more girls, just more of a social life. Instead of challenging myself in this new environment and trying to grow up, the more trouble I got myself into. The reason was obvious:

- I had a job so that meant I had money I could blow and hang out with.
- I had just been approved for my very first apartment so I could invite anyone over without having to abide by anyone's rules.
- I was meeting more women and was starting to hang out in the city more often.

Because of the above reasons, I lost focus on what I should be doing. I wasn't paying any bills on time and I started missing work because I was partying all the time wasting my money and not getting much rest. All it was doing was hurting me because nothing meant more to me than the city life. After only two months in my apartment, I broke my lease and left the rental property without giving notice, moving in with my high school friend. I could not afford the rent because of the poor decisions I was making, and because of my inability to prioritize correctly. I had no sense of direction and I was heading down the wrong path again but this time I was on my own. My determination was to live the life I had always envisioned for myself and

My Lack of Ambition

that vision was that of a celebrity or a hustler. I wanted to be the person who spent money and drove the nicest cars—after all, I was at every club in town, talking to beautiful women and enjoying life, and that was the life I wanted all along. In reality, I had not obtained the ability to live this sort of lifestyle, so I fronted as if I did.

I used to see women attracted to men who drove nice cars and paid good money to get into the nicest and most elite clubs in the city. Because the women liked that, that's what I wanted to portray. Even though I knew that, financially, I was not in a position to do that. I would save my money up until I had a thousand dollars and I would rent a car to imitate that life and if it got the attention of a beautiful woman, that's all that mattered.

Before this flamboyant lifestyle I was emulating would come to an end I wanted to find a woman who I could attract to be with so I wouldn't have to try to live like this. I could not just be myself because that would not get me the type of girls I wanted. That's when I came across a gorgeous woman named Erin. She was everything I was hoping to find in a woman. Erin was very caring and loving, and she always enjoyed being around me. The problem was that I knew it and took advantage of it. I knew I wanted her, but because I was in this big city, I still wanted more. Erin was different from most of women with whom I normally associated myself. She was the type of woman who would motivate me and push me to be the best person I could be—something that I needed but did not pay much attention to at the time. Her family embraced me and I started to see family as I had never seen it before. They were so close and I felt like this was the life I wanted, but I still could not remain focused enough to get it. I only thought that I wanted that life when I was around her family. Unfortunately, I was too far gone and there was no turning back from my devious ways at that point.

Erin and I had been together for a year. I began to notice myself becoming this controlling person. I wanted to know her every move and the company she hung around, as well as whom she'd be talking to on her phone. I was very spoiled and acted very insecure around her. I knew it was wrong but I did not care. I started to revert back to my childish ways acting spoiled and wanting my way all the

My Lack of Ambition

time. I noticed that Erin was trying her hardest to put up with my wrongdoings, but it was too much for her to bear (like they say, when a woman is fed up there is nothing a man can do). After months of emotional abuse, Erin had enough. Because of my controlling and determined ways, I would not let her go. I repeatedly started calling her and showing up uninvited to her home to her surprise. When I realized I was losing her, I wanted to be with her even more. Sometimes a person does not realize a good thing until it's gone. I got so out of control and tried so hard to keep her from leaving that she had to involve her mother. It would be times when I would call and her mother would have to answer her phone and threaten me to leave her daughter alone. After seeing that I knew I had gone too far. I had become this out of- control young man who seriously needed a reality check. I never cared about a person like Erin up to that point so I didn't know how to channel my emotions. After that relationship ended, and I had healed emotionally, I started working very hard on myself so that I would never be a control freak or a spoiled individual like that again. I took time out for myself and did not involve myself in a serious relationship with any woman for a few months. I wanted to become a decent man and set an example on being respectful toward women. Of course that did not happen in the least.

My behavior was influenced by what I saw around my neighborhood, as I grew up. Whether it was my uncles, my brothers, or the average Joe I saw in the streets, none of them had a worse effect on me than my cousin John. John had been living in Atlanta for a couple of years before I got there. He knew things about the city I would never have discovered on my own. He knew all the hottest spots and where the nicest girls hung out. After breaking up with Erin, I started hanging out with my cousin and we began to do the things I was trying to refrain from, which was hanging out at the best clubs and chasing women.

My cousin's idea of a great time was meeting women and seeing just how many he could sleep with. His statement to me was, "You are not trying to marry these hoes, just meet them and sleep with them." That was obviously something I had been doing for a while, but I was trying to change. As long as I was with John, change was not going

My Lack of Ambition

to happen. My behavior was influenced by my cousin as an adult. I would watch him tell women just about anything, and they would believe it time and time again. The difference between John and I was that he did not have a job, but he would always dress nice. He would say to me, "Just because you don't have money doesn't mean you can't look like you got money." That was a technique I would use for many years.

After hanging out and perfecting how to use women like John, I would have women buy me things and pay off my debts. I would drive their cars, borrow money from them, and sometimes stay with them. I was terrible—my word was no good and I was very inconsistent, but convincing. I did not take the blame for anything I did wrong. One thing I did have was a conscience. I knew the things I was doing to those women were wrong but because of my surroundings— and by that I mean John—I didn't stop. John had become a terrible influence on me. The more women I saw John with, the more women I wanted. It started to become a contest between us. I was trying my best to keep him from being able to claim that he had been with more women than I had. We had fun, but after a while it became pathetic. ***The more women I met, the more women got hurt.***

When I was 26 I started to realize that I needed to make a change in my approach with women. I had to stop telling them only what they wanted to hear, knowing that I was lying. I also needed to stop trying to convince them that I was that special guy they were looking for; that just wasn't true. I started meeting established, successful women who only wanted men to be honest with them. Because my life wasn't good and I did not have anything to offer a woman but lies, meeting mature women who were very accomplished made me feel intimidated due to their success. If I did have the courage to approach her it was only with lies because I thought if my qualifications were not good enough, she would not accept me. At 26 being myself was extremely difficult.

> - **I didn't have my own place to live because I couldn't afford one on my own.**
> - **I didn't even own a car I was riding the bus system called Marta.**

I could not compete with the image that most people in Atlanta portrayed. So I just lied my way into the lives of these ladies.

By the time a woman realized that my life was a lie, I'd already gotten what I wanted out of her—sex, money, and gifts. It was sad to see how a woman felt after being used. What was even sadder was that I did not even care. I was never going to see those women again. What I didn't know was that I had ruined their trust in men and had reinforced the stereotype about men which was, that men are dogs and there are no good men out there. My attitude was that it wasn't my problem to fix and the next man she came across could deal with her issues. I could not care less about their feelings.

Derrick Taylor

In 2002 at the age of 27, I met Jennifer. Physically, this young lady had everything I desired in a woman. She had beautiful eyes, beautiful hair, a gorgeous smile, and most of all—a nice body. I immediately wanted one thing from her, just as I did with many other women because I refused to fall for her because of my situation with Erin. That did not last long; this woman had my nose wide open. All I wanted was to spend as much time with her as possible. Everything between us moved quickly from kissing on the first date, to engaging in sex within a few days after meeting her. I was introduced to her parents after a week of meeting her. Eventually we would spend every weekend together. I started thinking she was the one but only from a physical perspective. She was beautiful, the sex was great, and that's all that mattered to me. I started hanging out with all of her friends and she even started spending nights at my place. I would do just about anything for this girl—I thought it was love at first sight.

During our sexual encounters I would ask her to have my baby in the middle of sex, and she would respond, "Yes." She may not have meant it, but I took her literally

My Lack of Ambition

and proceeded to conceive a baby, despite that we were not married and had no careers. What the heck, I did not care. I was going to be with that girl and if it took a baby to make that happen, so be it. A month later we learned that we were indeed having that baby. Jennifer cried, but I was overcome with joy. After a while of celebrating that we had a baby on the way, reality hit me: I did not have any idea about how I was going to take care of a baby. I never had my father in my life so the only thing I could think of was how to stay in my child's life and not become like my own father.

During her pregnancy my focus shifted to the baby and my attention to Jennifer lessened. My womanizing ways started to affect our relationship. Realizing she was pregnant with my baby made me understand she would be in my life forever—at least, that's what I thought. Throughout the pregnancy I reverted back to being this controlling, insecure man who wanted all the attention and wanted things his way. I would pick fights with her, which stressed her out and made her not want to be around me. Around her parents we would act as if everything was great, but when we were alone together all hell would break loose. The more bad behavior I displayed, the further she pulled away. I could sense that her intentions were to have this baby and get away from me. I would blame all of our problems on her simply because she wouldn't listen to me. I saw myself becoming this terrible person. After six months of behaving badly towards her and only three months before the baby was due I needed to become a different person. Being afraid that I was losing the woman who was carrying my child was a terrible feeling. It never crossed my mind to propose and ask Jennifer to marry me. That was a commitment that I wasn't ready for, and marriage was not an option.

My son was born September 8, 2003. I was the proudest man in the world. Before I officially named my son, I wanted to name him after me. Throughout Jennifer's pregnancy I asked myself how I could give my child the name of a selfish womanizer who disrespected women and had no goals, no career, and expecting him to follow in my footsteps. This was a no brainer, so I named him after my oldest brother Michael, who helped me through so many situations in my life. As I looked into my sons eyes while

My Lack of Ambition

holding him in my arms I could only think about how to fix the problems I had and hope that I could make things right for him. I was making promises that I may not keep but the healing process had to begin.

If I wanted my son to follow in my footsteps and wanted to be a positive role model for him, I was would have to change my ways and become a real man. My biggest fear was becoming a deadbeat father who could not support his son or teach him how to become a decent, respectable man. I was convinced my change would start immediately. The next year I attempted to go back to school as the first step toward changing myself. I enrolled at Atlanta Metropolitan College to pursue my childhood dream of becoming a basketball coach. Basketball was something that I had always excelled in, and it was also something that held my interest. After two years of studies at AMC, I hit another obstacle. I had used up all of my financial aid, so I had no money to finish my studies. I was working at BellSouth but was not making enough, so I could not pay out-of-pocket for school.

Derrick Taylor

I put my college education on hold in order to get a second job so that I could make ends meet for my son. As a man who had the responsibility to do right by his son, I did what had to be done so that I could provide for my child. My second job was working as a janitor making $6.15 an hour, but the entire time I held that job, I was praying that this was not God's intent. Making very little money, I started borrowing money from my brother Michael, who already had to support his family. The bad decisions I had made in the past were catching up with me. I was headed in the wrong direction. Because of my situation, I had no other option but to hold onto that janitor job, which should have only lasted six months, I held for an entire year. Imagine having the opportunity to get a free education with a basketball scholarship, only to end up cleaning toilets for a living. I threw away a great opportunity I once had.

After a while, I began to lose hope. ***When a man loses hope he loses ground, he loses faith, and I had neither***. I did not understand what having faith meant. When I was a kid we always hoped that we could have things; we always hoped that we would get out of certain bad situations.

My Lack of Ambition

Growing up the way I did not having much, once I tasted a little bit of success I became accustomed to that finer lifestyle. I forgot my morals and values. I was lost. I had no guidance but that of Michael's. He did his best to try to keep me straight, but one can only teach a grown man so much. He would always tell me that my lifestyle would catch up with me and that I needed to stop living above my means. I did not listen. Despite experiencing many struggles and pain, I had not learned from my mistakes and the street life began to call to me again. This pattern seemed to always appear when I least expected it. Instead of trying to improve myself, get an education, and learn the importance of life, my lust for women overtook me again. I found myself repeating my mistakes; the only difference was that I had a son to raise.

Instead of it being about my son, it turned out to be about me. I started putting my son second to my own needs and desires—the deadbeat dad started to become a reality. This could not be, especially after the promises I made to my son about always being there for him. My son was now becoming subject to my lies. I started thinking I was simply a sperm donor who helped create a baby that I could not raise. It's not as if I was ever taught how to be a great dad—I'd never even met my own father. What I do know is that kids need comforting. I had to figure out how to bring that comfort into my son's life. I started thinking that maybe having a child was a mistake. My priorities were not where they needed to be. I started to make excuses and come up with lies that kept me away from my son. Weeks would go by without me seeing him. I would tell Jennifer lie after lie—"I have to work late," or "My car isn't running well." Yet when it was time to go to the club, I was ready at a moment's notice. It had become a habit to me, and it was easy because no matter what, I knew that my child's mother would always provide the nurturing that he needed. Because of that, it was easy to walk out of my child's life. I was running from responsibilities. I would decide when I wanted to see my son. I was becoming pathetic and both sides of the family began to notice, my family and hers. I was the ultimate worst when it came to being a father. I was a disgrace. I had no one to turn to because no one

My Lack of Ambition

trusted me. I had lied myself too far into a hole that I could not get myself out of it. I knew I needed to change.

In 2006 now 31, I became close to a young lady I worked with at Bell South named Carrie. Carrie was not normally the type of woman I would date—she was attractive but was not light-skinned and did not have that exotic look I liked—but she was special in her own way. I never knew how to be a man; she taught me the importance of being a great man in a relationship. Aside from Michael, Carrie was the only person who knew how to motivate me. She was determined to do well and that rubbed off on me. Carrie drove a nice BMW X5 SUV and she owned several real estate properties. She was willing to open that life up to me, and because of that I learned a great deal from her. In the time that we dated, I learned the importance of having good credit, saving money, and learned how to project a positive image, something that I had never considered. The most important thing she did was introduce me to God. I knew about God growing up as a child but having faith the way she did, and seeing the way she called on him was something I did not have, however, it interested me. I started attending church with her on a regular basis and started reading the Bible. I made a dramatic turnaround because of this woman, whether she knew it or not.

Now with all of that done and me knowing the Lord a little more, there was one skill I still lacked, and that was how to be a boyfriend—a quality I had never been able to grasp. The feelings I had for this woman were deep. Things started happening that I would never have dreamed about. I experienced my first trip outside the United States with Carrie—we took a wonderful trip to the Bahamas together. Under her guidance my credit improved and I could now purchase a nicer vehicle. I went from having a 1992 Honda Accord to a 2003 Ford Explorer. Everything was going great and I thought I had everything I'd always wanted. After all the success I had in that year, you would think I'd grown up some. God had been good to me and I had a great woman in my life. The problem was I still lacked the knowledge on how to treat women that had been good to me. When I got my new car, I let it go to my head. I lost focus on my relationship with Carrie. I turned out not to be the man that she desired. Our relationship lasted about five

My Lack of Ambition

months. The breakup was difficult because I knew I had a great woman because of the change I saw in me. I thought that breaking up with a woman who at first wasn't my type would not bother me but it did. Because of her, I learned to look within when meeting that special woman. From that point on appearances were not as important to me.

The demise of that relationship led to my resolve to never again become deeply involved with a woman. Relationships to me at that point were slim to none; I could care less about them, but I still wanted that sexual pleasure. Women became a steppingstone for me, because I was never going to be hurt again. My goal was to break their hearts before they broke mine. I never thought one woman who broke my heart could have so much effect on how I treated the next woman, but she did. I never realized that the way I was treating her was wrong. Because I was selfish I never thought that I was hurting her feelings. All my life it was always about me, and only me. I never grew out of that need for attention.

It is so disappointing to see a person give you their heart only for someone to stomp all over it. That's exactly what I was doing and I did not have a care in the world. If I were going to live this life it was something I would have to take advantage of—what an attitude to have. Just as they say women sometimes use what they got to get what they want, I would think, "Here I am, this handsome young man that women like and are attracted to— I can do the same." In turn, that's exactly what I did. I had to figure out how to get to the top, so I started taking advantage of more women allowing them to think we were in a relationship and ending it once I had gotten what I wanted from them. I had become this great big scum of the earth. It became clear to me that time was passing me by and my life was not going to get any better. The only thing I had going was a great lying game. I thought I wanted to learn my lesson and become a great man and also be in a committed relationship. I may have wanted that but I was not ready for that.

To love someone else you have to love yourself and the most important thing is to love God first. I never knew how to love myself, so I could never love another woman. Throughout my life I treated women as though they were nothing, and as if they were beneath me because I did not

My Lack of Ambition

love myself, nor did I have the relationship with God that I should have been seeking. The only time I remember going to church was while I was dating Carrie. When I wasn't dating, I would never wake up and say, "Hey, I'm going to find a church home and try to become a better person." If I met a woman and she went to church I pretended to be interested in going with her just to gain her approval and be with her. I would become this God-fearing man overnight in order to make to her think I was into church. If that is not one-step from hell I don't know what is. As sad as that may sound, it was easy to accomplish. My infidelities in relationships were a must have, and no relationship was going to work if it were left solely up to me. I was going to ruin as many lives as possible.

When it came to improving my life, I had every excuse in the world to do otherwise. I was content with making a little money and living paycheck to paycheck. I could care less if my life made a dramatic turnaround. I was paying $400 dollars in child support now, thinking that I was taking care of my child, adjusting my wages and realizing that after child support was paid I still had enough left to live and hang out at night. Week after week, month after month, I accrued more debt because I was still living above my means. I was in a no-win situation. Child support had to be paid and I still had to live. I was becoming desperate. I had nowhere to turn. It got to the point where I didn't even care about my life. It was just as if I were that child again, always trying to get attention. I felt as if no one cared about me. I could not call on anyone for help because of my lack of credibility. I started feeling sorry for myself. I had become a big joke to myself and was unreliable to my family—not even they could trust the things that I said. I was giving up on life.

I did not know what the purpose of a man was. Growing up I thought I knew. To be honest, I thought I knew it all. I didn't know anything. The most I knew was that a man is to have a job, support his family, and just live life to the fullest. I thought, in my situation, one out of three was not bad. My idea was to live life to the fullest and grab every opportunity to do what it took to be happy, which in some cases would not always be the right thing to do. That was the only thing I did. I forgot about the real essence of

My Lack of Ambition

life and about how to respect the people in my life and how to set an example of a real man. Overall, I was not a great person.

I did not know how to accept that other people had feelings, too. That was not my concern. All that mattered to me was that I got what I wanted. At this point in my adult life, the purpose of a man was to simply survive. I had nothing I could call my own so for me I was only existing. If I were to meet a great woman, I had nothing to offer her. No woman would want a man with no goals, no motivation, no respect for his surroundings, and most of all, one who did not understand what it took to be a man. Sometimes I would ask myself why I was even alive. Here I was, this man who'd had so many opportunities to finish school, play the sport that he loved, and have a great life. I lacked focus and ambition. I was always running. I thought it was too much work to look for a solution to my problems; it seemed like a waste of time. I had thrown away every opportunity I had that could have kept me from getting me in the dump I found myself in.

Derrick Taylor

When a man starts feeling bad for himself, he becomes hopeless. I was that man. I was not concerned about what was happening to me or what people thought of me. I was at the lowest point of my life. When people saw me they could not tell I had any problems that needed attention; I hid it so well. I had never trusted any woman growing up. If I had, maybe my life would have been easier. Maybe I could have been married by now, raising a great family and being a decent, hard-working man. That wasn't the reality of my situation. If I had learned to put my trust in God and treated the people who were a part of my life with respect maybe my life would be different. Your goal should be to learn from your mistakes and try not to make the same mistake twice.

MORAL

In this chapter I discussed the people I betrayed and disappointed. I took advantage of situations when it did not require for me to do so. Always know that when people are trying to help you never take advantage of them. Never bite the hand that can put you in better situations. Never use

My Lack of Ambition

people for what they have, rather embrace them and always remain humble because you never know if you will need that person again. To all the fathers, always strive to be a part of your child's life.

Man Up!

Life Is What I Made It

Chapter 8

Life Is What I Made It

> *"Never put off for tomorrow what you can do today. Tomorrow is never promised to you. Remember always that if you play now you will suffer later. Always put your responsibilities first and everything else will follow. You may think you have everything you want until something you need comes along."*
>
> ~D. Taylor

8

Life Is What I Made It

I was afraid of a good woman because I feared I would not live up to her expectations. I believed that I would become a disappointment to a good woman due to my unfaithful nature. I did not know how to separate who I was in the past from what I could become, still thinking that I could be a good man to a good woman. I had become so materialistic that I assumed that I had to have the nicest car, the finest girl, and all the perks that came with that lifestyle. I thought I needed those things in order to find that special woman. I was very simple-minded and only looked at life through the lens of material things. The more I tried to obtain those things the further behind I got in my true priorities. I did not want a spiritual woman or a woman with great morals—appearances were all that mattered. I did not care about her intellect or what she had going for herself, the only thing that mattered to me was that she looked good.

The girls I liked did not like me in the same way. They cared only about money and material items. The little money that I did have I spent on women as though I were a baller. I could not save money to save my life. I fronted as if I had everything in the world but I was living this fantasy lifestyle that I could only maintain for a short period of time. I thought if I had those material things that the type of girl I was interested in would give me a chance. In other words I thought I was playing them, but in actuality they were playing me. Finances were my main topic when I was surrounded by women. The discussions would lead to where I could take her and what I could do for her. I never considered that this might not be what she wanted, but if I were stupid enough to blow my money on her, she wasn't going to stop me. When the funds ran out, she ran out.

I lied about the smallest things, not thinking that I would have to live that lie for the duration of the relationship. I was basically living life like a movie script: boy meets girl, boy lies to girl, loses girl, and then moves on. It became a pattern. It had gotten so bad women could immediately tell what I was about as soon as they met me. I was this loud, arrogant man who had a little boy's mentality. I became an easy target for a woman who wanted someone to spend money on her because I made it so obvious that I would do just that. My brother used to always say, "Man, what type of women do you mess with?" I would quickly respond that the women I messed with did everything I wanted, but he knew I was lying because I could never keep any money on me; I was always broke. I would even ask him for money to take these women out. I thought the only way to get a decent, classy woman was to have a large amount of money.

After a while I had no more money to spend on girls, and no money to help me enjoy my life. I finally faced reality and admitted that I had a serious ego problem and problems with dishonesty. Only then could I admit the problems I had and become a great man and have a great woman. I had no clear image of what a real man was. I was confused on how to be responsible. If things did not directly benefit me, I wanted no part in them. I used to hear the saying, "You learn from your mistakes and you move on." I always moved on but I never learned from my mistakes. Therefore, I could not progress due to my lack of focus. I began to think that, no matter what I did, I was always going to be stuck in the life I had made for myself. I thought I would never be able to have a family of my own and that I would never be successful in anything. I was never the type of man to think about his future. I was living in the moment, and my moment was going to be hanging out at the hottest clubs and being with the prettiest women. That's all I knew and I did not think any of that was going to change.

Think about this: Men today have to step it up notch. We cannot have our strong men not taking responsibility for their actions. A man is every bit the leader of his house. A woman seeks a strong man, a man who is a caring provider and a leader. The most important thing to know is that a man has to have God in his life. God is the answer to all problems. A man who seeks God is a man who can lead his family in the right direction. A man of God seeks a supportive woman who is warm and understands how to let a man

Life Is What I Made It

be a man, a woman who knows how to raise her children to be good, kind-hearted human beings who respects the family unit. Men have to understand how to be a role model for their children because children look to their father for guidance and support. A man should always stay strong for his family, stand tall, and accept that he can be dedicated. No matter what the circumstances if a man has God in his life and is faithful to his family, nothing can tear that family apart. A man should set an example for his children so that they know they can count on him. A real man admits his faults, and looks for ways to resolve his problems. No matter what, a man has to stay dedicated to his family and always put their needs ahead of his own. A positive home is always a happy home. A man should never put anything before his family. The most important thing for a man is to live God's word to the fullest.

After all the adversity I faced having no one to turn to, I had to seek God. I did not know how to go about it. When I did go to church, my body was there but my mind sure was not. I could hear the pastor preaching the Word of God, but I could never comprehend any of it. I did not understand what that meant or what purpose it served me. The main reason I was at church was to say that I attended. I was not learning a damn thing. I could see how people reacted to certain messages, how they would jump to their feet and praise the Lord, but it was just funny to me. I never volunteered to help at the church. To be honest I never even had a steady church home. I would bounce around from church to church, hoping that I would gain some kind of understanding. Reading the Bible was never an option. I only picked up the Bible when I knew I would be going to church. I started to question God's existence. If there was a God, I surely didn't understand why I was struggling with so much and treating people so poorly. I was lying, cheating, and being this nasty person with a huge ego problem and no respect for anyone. I had no faith, and did not even bother to seek God.

Church was never an integral part of my life growing up, and I had made it this far, so I did not think I needed God. I did not think he could make changes in my life. Whenever people would speak about the Lord around me, I would always come up with excuses and get very defen-

Life Is What I Made It

sive—I did not want to hear that stuff. It did not help to be around family that always spoke about church but did not actively try to live a Godly life. I could not trust their word. They were nothing but hypocrites to me. They would discuss their feelings about God and the church, and they would immediately go back to chasing girls and drinking. To be honest, when I went to church my only objective was to see what type of women were there and what they were wearing. I was just an extra body, taking up space. I did not affiliate myself with church-going people—I didn't want that lifestyle to rub off on me. I stopped believing and the less I heard about church, the better. I used to hear all the time that prayer is powerful and can help you with everything if you have faith. I tried that and none of my prayers were answered, at least not in the way that I thought they should have been. So ultimately I just quit going to church.

Nothing seemed to get better. People started to ask me, "Why are you single? What do you do in your free time?" My answer would be, "I'm not looking for a woman and I do absolutely nothing in my spare time." I started not wanting anyone in my life. I was so content to be alone that when the weekends would arrive, I would just lock myself away in my apartment, without even trying to see friends or family. By doing this, I knew I couldn't hurt or disappoint anyone. I began to figure out who I was as a person and had to stop blaming my problems on everybody else. Until I figured out a solution, there was no way I could let myself get involved with or be around anyone. Most people thought I was being self-centered and assumed I thought highly of myself. I knew that wasn't what I was doing, but I did not bother to correct anyone.

I hardly had any friends. I substituted my brothers and my cousin John as my friends. At times, I would try to get away from my family for a while. In reality they were what I needed; they understood me best. I could take advice from them and acknowledge that they knew better than I did. When I thought life had become a no-win situation, I did not want to be alive because I was always in denial, never regaining focus and never believing in myself. Never knowing whom my father was I started to wonder if maybe I had inherited my bad traits from him. I had no way of knowing. I never tried to improve myself. I could make my

Life Is What I Made It

life appear to be a blessing to others, but in reality that was a cover up of who I was. When things would get a little better, I would quickly forget how I got that far and have a total relapse.

My family could see the dramatic change in my life. Any help they tried to give me I took for granted. I was the type of person who could not sit still long enough to gather my thoughts. Instead of turning to my family for help I turned back to the thing I knew best: the streets. I felt comfortable hanging out late at night. This was freedom to me. Eventually I became a regular in the party crowd again, this time nothing too fancy. I tried to keep it on the lower-budget side of things. I would only go to places that I knew I could afford. I would still blow five hundred dollars in one night at one club. Knowing that was all of the money I had, I still did not hesitate. I was always telling myself that money comes and goes, not thinking that I had bills to pay. As far as my bills, I would always come up with some excuse for why I could not pay a certain bill on time. I would constantly call the bill collectors to request an extension, just so I could have money for the nightlife.

Derrick Taylor

My priorities were so jacked up that I would go to the club before I paid my bills. I would even be late on paying my rent sometimes, just so I could have some fun. I had no idea how deep of a hole I was digging for myself. When I needed money, I would ask my brother if I could borrow some from him. I knew I could always count on Michael to loan me the money. I would tell him that I needed to pay a bill by a certain day or that my rent was going to be late and I was going to be evicted if I did not pay. Sometimes it worked and sometimes it didn't. When he did loan me the money I would call my cousin and say to him, "Let's do it again," meaning "Let's get into the streets and spend the ten or twenty dollars I just got from my brother." Knowing that I could rely on my brother, I knew I could waste the money I borrowed and still be alright when I needed more.

Having a place to live is one thing, but having a place you cannot afford is another. I lived in places I knew I could not afford because I was trying to impress people who could care less about what I had. Life is about the choices you make, and I chose to live as though I was the man, but on a budget that couldn't pay for anything. I was the type of guy

Life Is What I Made It

who would sit at home watching BET, wanting to live the lifestyle I saw on those shows. I was a grown man physically, but a young boy at heart.

Things got more confusing by the day. My problem was that all my life I wanted attention. I wanted respect, but I lacked focus, and I was out of control. I did not know how to talk to people. I could never get along with anyone except my family. Even then I had to work extremely hard to regain their trust. People figured out what type of person I was as soon as we met. I had no inner peace and I was not a man of God, nor did I even believe or have faith that things could get better. My mother was only three hours away, but I did not visit her as often as I should have. Whenever birthdays and holidays would come around I was so broke that I could not get anyone a gift. I became a ghost during those times. The easiest thing about my life was that I could disappear when it came time to celebrate other peoples' lives. *I was a straight user and a leech, and I tried my best to suck everything I could out of people.*

*****

Derrick Taylor

Derrick's Truth: I remember working with an older co-worker at BellSouth and not having enough money to pay my rent. I begged and promised her that if she gave me three hundred dollars I would pay her back. I never thought I was capable of taking advantage of a sweet old woman. I dodged this woman until she realized that I had no intention of paying her back. Feeling disgusted with myself I wanted to quit my job. At that point, all I could think about was how my uncles took advantage of my grandmother in that same way—borrowing money and never repaying her. I had to do something. Concerning this co-worker, I started giving her 10 dollars here and there until she finally told me to keep the money. To me that was like winning the battle, but it showed how selfish I was to take advantage of a woman who was so sweet and who had the decency to believe in me. I vowed to never hurt anyone again and try to seek help for myself. Sometimes I would become extremely stressed out because I could not fight the overwhelming emotions that I had. I was fighting a demon I could not defeat, which was myself. My poor decisions and my bleak outlook on life had affected me.

*****

MORAL

In this chapter I mention not putting my priorities first. I discussed how I always lived above my means. You should never portray to be something that you're not. Create a solid foundation that can never be broken. If people do not like you for who you are, they are not for you. Always have business about yourself, meaning take care of the little things that are important. Just be yourself and don't do anything you do not feel like doing in order to please someone else.

Man Up!

My Brother's Keeper

Chapter 9

My Brother's Keeper

> *Wise words from my brother:*
>
> *"Everybody keeps telling me to stop saving you, because you keep living above your means. You continue to do the same old shit and you're not trying to change. You constantly lie about unnecessary shit. It's going to take something drastic to happen before you realize you're not fooling anybody but yourself. I don't want anything from you. All I ever did was try to help you. I'm so disgusted with you and your mentality that I don't want to call or even talk to you. You think life is a damn joke, man. There are so many people you've lied to that no one likes dealing with you. As God be my witness, I will help you this time, but you will drown from this point forward. It's your life, so do as you damn well please."*
>
> ~M. Taylor

9

My Brother's Keeper

> *Everybody has a role model within themselves. Search your soul to be the best role model for yourself and others will follow. Serve as an example of transformation as you journey through your life. If you choose to follow the example of another, make sure the steps you follow are those of a true and honest individual.*
>
> *~D. Taylor*

Every child grows up with a role model or at least wanting one. My role model was my older brother, Michael. He was the type of guy who did what it took to survive. For most children, growing up without much seems like a failure; to Michael it was pure motivation something that I was sorely lacking. Out of four boys in the house, it would seem reasonable to think that at least one of them would try to make something of themselves and work to set an example for the rest, that was Michael. My mother spoiled my younger brother Tony and me, but Michael did not have that spoiled mentality.

Michael had a good head on his shoulders and knew he wanted to try to provide for himself. At the young age of 13 he would find different jobs to do around the neighborhood so he could make money to buy his own clothes. He essentially maintained and supported himself from the age of 13 into his adulthood. He was never provided with the kind of help from our mother which I received. He learned how to be a man when he was still a boy. I remember seeing Michael and his friends being picked up by a White man in a big white pickup truck every day, wondering where they were going. Every Friday afternoon he would show me at least two hundred dollars that he had earned from working everyday with this man. "Man," I would say, "What are y'all doing and how can I get money like that?" My brother had a way of getting what he wanted because he was such a likeable person; I, on the other hand, got along with hardly

My Brother's Keeper

anyone. Willingly, my brother talked the man into letting me work for him. As we headed to the rural side of town, I started to see huge fields full of tomatoes, corn, and many other kinds of vegetables. We would jump off the back of the truck and work in these big fields. The White man we worked for was a very nice old man. He would give us meals throughout the day as we worked. Honestly, the only downside to this deal was how hot it would get. Sometimes the temperature would reach near 100 degrees.

After one week, I enjoyed my first paycheck. Making my own money was a wonderful feeling. Each week the amount would range from one hundred to two hundred dollars. I was making decent money despite being younger than my brother; however, I had to give my money to my mother because I was too young to even cash a check. She would cash my check and save the money so I would not lose it. My brother saved just about every penny he earned. If I'd had half the knowledge and sense that he had, I would have become a much better man. I had plenty of opportunities to be like my brother, but I never took advantage of them. I watched him turn into this great man with goals and direction that helped him keep his head above water, and although he had two other brothers he would always make time to try to teach me everything he knew. Just like him, I was very good at sports, which helped us create an even closer bond. Whatever sport he played, I played. My other siblings thought Michael showed favoritism towards me because he invested more time with me instead of them, but I did not care. I felt as though I was important to Michael, and that was something I desperately needed as a young boy. I thought I was going to be just like him.

In 1991, Michael went off to college. I was left at home trying to follow in his footsteps-something I was never able to do. I thought it would be easy to live up to the example he set and the knowledge he had passed on to me. The truth was, once he left and was out of my daily life, I took a turn for the worse. It became evident that I did not have the heart or the determination that he possessed. It turned out that I desperately needed him around to motivate me to live up to the same expectations he had.

My Brother's Keeper

People started to tell me that I would never be like my brother and I would never make a name for myself. People always related to me as "the little brother." They would never say my name; they would just call me "Michael's little brother." I began feeling like my brother's shoes were too big to fill, his footsteps were overwhelming to me. I stopped working hard and no longer pushed myself to do my best. I was quickly becoming a lazy person, wasting my potential without a care in the world. Life began to move in slow motion; everything I started only got half done. People rarely asked me to be a part of something because everyone knew I was not going to give my best effort toward anything. When it came time to go to basketball camp with my team, I was not allowed to participate because no one believed in me.

When Michael had a break from class, he would call to check up on me. Every time he did call he would ask me how everything was going. I lied to him and told him everything was going well. I acted as if he did not know the truth about me already, forgetting that my brother was a household name in Statesboro. He had ways of discovering just about anything he wanted to know about anyone in town. When I would tell him lies about making good grades and staying out of trouble, he would pause and start laughing at me as if I were a joke. He would always say one line that I knew meant that he knew the truth: "Man, are you kidding me?" My response was always the same, "What?", as if I was totally innocent and did not know what he meant.

The goals he set I would never reach or take seriously. I had messed up so many opportunities that my word was not reliable. I had no will to do anything that took effort. I always depended on others to do everything. ***A man who cannot be trusted is a man who has no knowledge of faith or the sense of what it takes to be responsible toward anything or anyone***. I can admit that I listened very hard and tried to follow the instructions he gave me. They motivated me; Michael's answers were words to live by. I would soak them in like a sponge but reality would always fall back into my lap. When I look back throughout my life, and realize how much he helped me and how much he tried to be there for me, it made me feel blessed to have him as a brother.

MORAL

In this chapter I explained my brother as being a role model in my life. I never took any accountability for what he was telling me on how to improve myself. If a person has a positive influence in your life and who is trying to motivate you to do the right thing, that is advice one should embrace. If a person provides you opportunities for change accept it.

Man Up!

Forever In My Heart…R.I.P

Chapter 10

Forever In My Heart…R.I.P

> *Everyone has that special person whom they truly care about and miss when they are gone. If that's the case, tell the one you love how much you love them and care for them while they are still here. It's a shame how many people wait until it's too late to say how they really feel about someone. Never be ashamed to tell someone how you feel, because you never know when it will be the last time.*

10

Forever In My Heart…R.I.P.

The only woman I ever knew I could trust was my grandmother. What a sweet woman she was. I would do anything and everything for her. I thought no one had a better relationship with my grandmother than I did. I remember how she would wake up early in the morning, make us breakfast, my favorite were her pancakes because she would make her homemade syrup that I loved so much. We would get dressed and my siblings and I would go out into her garden she had planted in the backyard and pick corn, tomatoes, peas, and collard greens. We would pull weeds, feed the chickens and dogs, and help her fertilize and water the garden. I learned everything about how to tend to a garden; I had a daily lesson.

Sometimes my grandmother would send us to IGA, the neighborhood grocery store. She would write down on a list all the items she needed from the store and give the list to my older brother because she thought I would lose it. I had a bad reputation for losing things. I would get upset every time, but she had this way of involving me so that I would feel as if I were contributing. She would ask me to check off the items on the list as my brother collected them. I felt very important. When we would get back home, she would have these huge white buckets full of peas and corn, and she would ask us to shuck the vegetables into a pot. That was the only thing I did not like because it generally became an all-day thing. It was for my grandmother, so I agreed. I remember having a full head of hair on my head, and my grandmother would sit me down on her lap and braid my hair. I did not like it because the neighborhood children would pick on me and call me a girl. I would run back to the porch and ask her to take the braids out because my friends were making fun of me. Once again, my grandmother always had her way of making me feel good. She would tell me that those children were not my friends; real friends would not pick on me. That always comforted me

Forever In My Heart...R.I.P.

and I would soon be up and back out the door to play with my friends again.

I never saw my grandmother upset. I never recall her having one angry bone in her body. She welcomed her home to any of the other children in the neighborhood and feed them. The only bad thing I do remember was the way my uncles acted around her. Boy, they were terrible. They ate up everything in the house, always borrowed money from my grandmother and never paid her back, and they never cleaned up after themselves because they expected my grandmother to do it. They would come into the house at all hours of the night, and they would even fight with each other around her. I did not approve of this, but I could not say anything fearing they would whip me when my grandmother wasn't looking. She would always tell me, "Do not grow up to be like your uncles. Theirs is an example you should not follow. When you grow up, do the complete opposite." My uncles were a bad influence on me. They would use drugs in the house, and sometimes even have the nerve to bring women home, though I did not mind the women because I would take a peak in their room to see what they were doing.

When I was 21 I started to notice changes in my grandmother's health. One thing I noticed was that sometimes she would have trouble walking on her own. I did not know why at the time, but it seemed very strange to me. I noticed her starting to depend on others more, however, she still had that fight in her. She went from walking around on her own to walking with a cane. When I would visit I would insist on helping her, but she would always respond that she did not need my help. The only thing she would let me do was get the door for her. Because she could not move around like she used too, it was strange to see her get out of bed later in the day rather than her usual time. Most mornings she would get up as early as six, now it would be nine in the morning before she got up. Later, I found out that the results of my grandmas health issues were due to cancer.

What I regret: I regret that when I got out of high school I stopped going to see my grandmother. I believed I had more important things to do, for example, hanging out with my friends, playing basketball, and going to the clubs. My mother used to tell me that she would ask about me but as long as I did not hear that she was doing badly and if she did not call on me to come by to do her a favor, I figured she was doing just fine. I regret the lies I remember telling my grandmother when I finally started returning to visit her. The lies I would tell her when she would ask me certain questions. One question in particular she would ask me was; why haven't I been by to see her. My response was that I had been away at college. I felt that I could get away with that lie because it involved me doing something with my life and I thought she would understand. I could not believe that I had lied to my grandmother. The lie was so easy, and I made her feel so proud of me that I couldn't tell her the truth, which was, that I dropped out of college. The thought of me being in college and becoming better than my uncles pleased her—so I ran with it.

*****

Derrick's Truth: I remember in August 2002 as I was heading up the street to catch the bus to go to work, my cell phone rang. It was my brother telling me something that I never thought I would hear—the call that no one ever wants to receive about a loved one.

"Hey man, what's up?"

"Nothing, I'm headed to work."

"Well I'm calling you to let you know that Mama—(that's what we called her), is gone."

"What do you mean, gone," I replied.

"She passed away."

*****

Damn, my mouth dropped and I could not believe it. I hadn't seen this woman in a long time and the first thing I thought of was the lie I told her about being in college. I felt awful and there was no way I was going to shake this off my conscience. I was devastated. This was the woman who raised me for all intents and purposes, and I could not even make time to visit her on a regular basis. I could not tell my own grandmother who raised me that I loved her for everything she had done. When we buried my grandmother, all I could think about were my last words being a

Forever In My Heart...R.I.P.

lie. I knew at that moment that I could not tell anyone I loved them if I couldn't even tell my own grandmother I loved her.

They say only a father can raise a boy to become a man. In my case, the values I did learn came from my grandmother. I think about all the little things we did together when I was young, from waking up early in the morning to planting a garden, or just helping her around the house. My grandmother worked so hard to strengthen my character and teach me to work well with others. Those lessons may have been simple, but to me it made a difference when it came to living life to the fullest. She was always working to groom me into a decent young man, a man who would know the importance of life and how to handle certain situations. As a child you don't think about that often, but life becomes a boomerang. What you lack in life it always comes back around to give you the reality check you need. My grandmother did the very best she could with me. All I had to do was soak in and follow the simple rules she taught. It wasn't a hard thing to do, but I just could not grasp it and live as she wanted me too. She offered me words of wisdom such as, treating people as you want to be treated, and whatever I wanted to be in life be the best at it. All she wanted me to do was follow her morals and try to understand the value of life. I miss her dearly, but I know she is in a better place now.

MORAL

This chapter is dedicated to my grandmother. I discuss how distant I became from her. Although I did spend much of my time with her growing up, I still felt as if I did not spend enough time as I should have. If there's a loved one that you are close too, never lose the bond that you have with them because you never know when it's thelast day you will ever see them again. Cherish every moment.

Man Up!

I Am All Grown Up

11

I Am All Grown Up

Today, I have found a church home with a strong, close-knit community. I fully believe that through God anything is possible. God helped me begin my search for answers to why I behaved terribly toward the women in my life. I always wondered why I was this unhappy, constantly depressed person. Through God the answer became perfectly clear to me: I did not love myself enough to even begin to love anyone else. I cheated myself, so I cheated others. I did not respect myself, so I didn't respect others. I controlled women and preyed on their weaknesses. If a woman tried to do me some good I chased her away; if a woman tried to stand up to me. I kick her out of my life.

Derrick Taylor

Through my walk with God I have learned to be more patient with women. I learned to give them the respect that they deserve. They say that a woman is the backbone and the emotional center of a family and that women love very strongly and very deeply. Men should always give women the utmost respect and love that they deserve. If I could take back anything from my past when it came to women, I would take back the lying, disrespectful, and hateful way I behaved toward them. I can see how much I have grown as a man over the years, and if I ever want to have that special lady in my life, I know I have to be considerate and respectful of her feelings, thoughts, and ambitions. I wish that no woman on earth should ever experience what I did to women. If a man is behaving disrespectfully toward a woman, she must stand up for herself and make it known that such behavior is unquestionably unacceptable. I pray to God that one-day I will find that special woman and finally be able to say those three important words: **I love you.**

MORAL

Now you know my story and several struggles I have encountered. It took me until I was in my thirties to figure out my life. I was always searching for answers, but the answers were within me. I had to do some soul searching to find those answers. I realized I had everything given to me only for me to throw it away. Had I been able to appreciate the opportunities I had, I would have been in a much better situation. I just did not know how to adapt to certain situations. I had numerous opportunities to better the lives of the people I betrayed and was dishonest to just by helping them in a time of need and I ignored those chances. ***Treat people the way you would like to be treated and Man Up to your mistakes!***

Man Up!

The Conversation About

Men and Women

12

The Conversation About Men and Women

What do men and women expect from each other?

Listen up, men. After sharing my story, which is full of difficult situations and environments, countless bad decisions, and a great deal of disrespect and abuse toward women, I started wondering what factors determine whether or not a relationship is successful and how we, as men, can achieve that kind of success. The first thing I knew was that whatever determines a happy relationship starts with our women. So I asked myself, "What is it that women want from men, for a man to be considered a great husband and, better yet, a great human being?" After talking to several women, I determined that most women want the following things:

1. Women want a man to be confident.

2. Women want a man who makes them feel like they are the only woman in the world.

3. Women want a man with a good sense of humor.

4. Women want a man who will listen to them.

5. Women want a man who will treat them like they are the sexiest woman he's ever seen.

6. Women want loyal men—they want to know you will be faithful.

7. Women want a man who is sensitive to their needs and the needs of others.

8. Women love a man with a plan; a man with ambition and goals.

9. Women want generous men. Don't be a tight wad; give the women in your life gifts every now and then to show her you are thinking of her.

The Conversation About Men and Women

10. Be a true friend. Most women want a man who is not only their lover, but also their best friend.

11. Women want to be loved despite their flaws, and need to be satisfied mentally, emotionally, and spiritually as much as they do physically.

12. Women appreciate a man who is creative. It shows that he challenges himself and is always thinking and looking for new ways to solve problems and experience life.

13. Women want a man who will offer her a sense of security. Women want to know that their partner will always be by their side, no matter what the situation.

So, to my fellas out there: if this is all that women want from us, why is it so hard for some of us to give them what they want and find that successful relationship? No one I asked, male or female, could answer this question with anything resembling a complete answer. Luckily, women can at least give us (mostly clueless) men an insight into the female mind. From them, I've learned that what women are looking for in a man can be generalized into four categories that explain the characteristics they find appealing.

1. **Confidence:**

    Most men either have no confidence or carry with them a false sense of confidence that they use to try to impress women. Women, just like men, want to see real confidence in a man's behavior and attitude, and they are sensitive to true confidence versus false bravado.

2. **Affection:**

    Showing affection is not solely a matter of physical contact or emotional connection, but a complex mix of the two. Women want to know that they are appreciated—everyone does—and this comes from affection and closeness as much as it does through any other aspect of a relationship.

3. **Security:**

    We live in an age where women can be truly independent. It is no longer true that a man must provide every-

The Conversation About Men and Women

thing for his woman, but most women still like for their man to provide them with a sense of security. Now, security means more than simply bringing home the bacon or standing up for her honor. A woman wants to know that her partner is going to work at least as hard as she is to get the good things in life. Paying your bills and being financially honest with a woman are two great ways to prove that you are stable and can help ensure security in your relationship.

4. **Understanding:**

Women are often stereotyped as overly emotional individuals; the truth is that all human beings are emotional, male and female alike. To be understanding means providing a shoulder to cry on, honest advice, and support during tough times. It is easy for us as men to overlook the little things that, when taken together, add up to being an understanding person. If your girlfriend is feeling moody, consider curling up under a blanket with her and watching her favorite television show together. Understanding is a vital component of a successful romantic relationship, and one that we men seem to struggle with the most.

Remember that every woman is different, and most women wouldn't appreciate their having desires generalized into the above four categories—I include them simply as food for thought for those men who may feel totally confused about women's desires. No human being is exactly the same as another, and you will no doubt find women who aren't looking for security or an understanding man. However, trying to be sensitive, confident, open to showing affection and stability, and trying to be emotionally open and understanding can only make you a better and more interesting man and, hopefully, a more appealing lover and partner.

Now that I have shared a little of what women may be looking for in a man, I'd like to address the ladies and talk about four things that men look for in a woman:

1. **Good Sex:**

    Let's not pretend that only men are looking for a capable and attentive sexual partner. Men want a partner who will be willing to share her affection physically

The Conversation About Men and Women

without intimidating him. Besides, you can find out if you even like touching him long before committing to a date. Ladies, don't be intimidated by a man's desire for good sex—after all, isn't that something you want, too?

2. **Healthy Appearance:**

   Instead of trying to mold your body into someone else's idea of beauty, it's important to appreciate your own unique shape and work to maintain your health by taking care of yourself and practicing good hygiene. You have no say in whether or not a man is attracted to you, but you do have control over your health.

3. **Trust:**

   Here, trust refers not just to a man's ability to trust that his woman won't cheat on him, but to his ability to come to you for his emotional needs as well. If a man thinks you'll listen to his problems and then immediately run off to Twitter to your friends about it, he won't feel that sense of trust necessary to develop a healthy relationship. So how do you show a man that you are trustworthy? Avoid gossiping to him about your friends. It may seem fun, and yes, it's sometimes necessary to blow off steam, but it will teach him that you are an understanding person and that you take the problems of the people you care about seriously.

4. **Sense of Humor**

Humor is a great icebreaker in many different situations. There will most certainly come a time in your relationship when a good joke will keep a minor disagreement from becoming a full-fl edged argument. And laughter is also a great aphrodisiac. Men will find your sense of humor—no matter how goofy—a serious turn-on.

No two men are alike, and the desired traits in a girlfriend will differ from man to man. However, you can bet that some combination of the above features will attract just about any man.

Man Up!

Blog: Question and Answers

13

Blog: Question and Answers

I am not an expert, so the chances of me being able to answer the questions I have posed correctly are slim to none. My approach to this section was to ask these questions of both females and males and see what the differences in their answers and opinions would be. So let's blog!

1. **Why is it that some women who are treated very poorly by their man continue to stay with him?**

   FEMALE: Because we think we can change them.

   Female: Some women allow it to happen; some women stay because of low self-esteem. A man will only go as far as you let him.

Male: Some people subject themselves to unnecessary pain and punishment. We have all faced trials and tribulations in relationships that tear at our heart and our soul.

Female: I let one treat me poorly over and over again because I loved him and I kept listening to his promises to change. Now I know that he is incapable of change and I wouldn't wish him on any sane woman.

2. **If you have been seeing a man for a while and you have not labeled your relationship as being "together" or "partners," what does it mean when a man tells you he is not ready? What is it he's not ready for?**

Male: Not ready for commitment!

Male: When no lines have been established and someone says something like that, it means that things have already moved into that "together" stage, whether the man likes it or not!

The Conversation About Men and Women

Female: Sorry, he's just not that in to you. Move on. Staying with him is only keeping your true love from finding you!

Male: He could be feeling you a lot and see a real future with you, but he might not feel ready to give up the single life just yet.

Female: Regardless, a person who cuts off something that isn't even there is a waste of time.

3. **Women are you more attracted to a man for what he has and who is he rather than the man himself? What if he is broke with swagger—would you still be interested? Or what if he had no swagger and was kind of corny, but had lots of money?**

   Female: I'm attracted to a man I can trust. I trust men who are financially responsible. They don't have to be rich, by any means, only rich in love!

4. **Men, are smart women intimidating?**

   Female: Smart women intimidate some men.

Male: Okay, a little, but it's kind of hot—very hot!

Female: Not sure many men will have the guts to answer this, but in some circumstances—yes.

5. **How do women know what a real man is?**

Male: It's not about whether you're a good man or woman but about being a good human being. We get caught up in the nonsense. When you love yourself, you can easily love others around you.

6. **Men, what do you look for in a woman? What are some characteristics you find appealing?**

Male: A strong, independent woman who can just be herself. Just keep it simple and sweet.

7. **Why do men cheat? If they aren't happy why can't they just tell their mate so they can either work on it or move on?**

Male: Men cheat for all sorts of reasons. Sometimes it is simply because they can do it or because the opportunity is available, sometimes it is because they have low self-esteem, are unhappy at home, or are afraid of commitment and are just seeking fun.

8. **Regarding friendship is it possible for a guy to simply be friends with an attractive woman, or is he always waiting on an opportunity to get in (literally)?**

Male: With an underlying current of sexual attraction already there, the intimacy of a true friendship is at some point bound to cause a man to cross the line. And even if he doesn't cross the line, he will most certainly test the boundaries.

9. **How long should a woman wait for a man to pop the question?**

Male: Anything more than one to two years is way too long. If he can't decide by then whether or not he loves, then tell him to hit the bricks. Many men are terrified of marriage and would prefer to live with their girlfriends, having all the benefits and no responsibility, or just keep dating with no real commitment.

Derrick Taylor

10. How long does it take for a man to introduce a woman to his family?

Male: There is no specific point in time that one must be introduced to their partner's family. The when, is completely determined by the two people involved.

Man Up!

Your Approach Determines Your Place

14

Your Approach Determines Your Place

Within minutes of observing you or interacting with you, a woman will place you into one of three categories.

1. **Creep:**

   The creep is attracted to a woman but doesn't have the courage to openly interact with her, so he hovers around her, just hoping something will just happen. He's the guy who traces her mailing address and sends anonymous letters. He's the guy at the bar who will stare from a distance and when he's drunk enough, approach her without a smile and try to make stiff, serious conversation. Hint: Women run away from the creep.

Derrick Taylor

1. **Lover:**

    The lover understands attraction. When he is interested in a woman and wants to spend time with her, he says, "I'm going to a wine-tasting workshop on Wednesday, would you like to come along?" What the woman hears is, "I'm already having a fun time without you. If you join me we can have fun together. But if you don't join me I'll still have fun." This is the kind of man that women desire sexually. Hint: Many women seek a provider type as a husband or boyfriend to pay the bills, while discreetly seeking a lover type on the side.

2. **Provider (a.k.a., husband material):**

    The provider is the type of guy who treats attraction like a business deal. He buys the woman dinners and gifts and hopes she'll have a relationship with him in return. But that's not exactly how it works. When a man asks a woman, "Can I take you out to dinner," what she hears is, "I cannot have fun without you, so I'd like to buy you some food and make you see me as a provider. Then, hopefully, you'll accept me and make my life ex-

Your Approach Determines Your Place

citing." Hint: Women usually don't have sex with the provider; they delay the sex until marriage. Even if you want a woman to see you as husband material, you have to first get her to see you as lover. It's easy to go from lover to husband, but not the other way around.

Man Up!

Let Your Intuition Guide You

15

Let Your Intuition Guide You

To all the men out there who are in search of that special someone or, better yet, have found that special relationship, I give you this to think about: When we become conflicted in relationships, it is often because our brain says one thing and our heart says another. We try to find a solution with our brains and react with our hearts. But the soul gets energy from both the mind and the heart; if we can learn to listen to our inner voice; our souls can be the arbitrator between the two. We must learn to listen, hear, and trust our soul's inner voice—it's never wrong.

If you have found a special lady but still aren't quite sure whether or not you are really in love with her, then read the list below and consider which of the statements apply to you.

- You are inspired to make her smile every day.
- You give her a gift and it fills you with happiness.
- You look in her eyes and feel a jolt of positive energy.
- You are inspired to make her feel safe and loved.
- You desire and are filled with joy from her affection.
- You do just about anything you can to take care of her.
- You are inspired to be the best you can be for her.
- You are dedicated to the success of the relationship.
- You look at her and know that you are home.
- You look at her and your soul is at peace

If at least half of this list applies to you, then you have done the necessary things to better yourself and become a great man. You have found your special lady and that successful, happy relationship we are all seeking. I look forward to the day when I meet that special woman and am finally able check off all of the items on the list.

Book Review

What Are Your Thoughts?

_____

_____

_____

_____

_____

_____

_____

_____

_____

_____

_____

_____

Acknowledgements

I would like to thank everyone that purchased Man Up: One Man's Sincere Regret for Sabotaging His Relationships and who have shown me continued love and support.

I want to thank Jessica Cage, who has worked with me on this project from the beginning until the end, translating my unique phrases, putting them on paper and making my message understandable to all that have read this book. In other words she had the abilities to make my thoughts quite enjoyable and pleasurable to read.

To my entire family, from the bottom of my heart, I say thank you. Thank you for your support, thank you for your understanding and thank you all for just listening to me.

Most importantly, thank you my heavenly Father who has given me every blessing I have ever had in my years of living. I am grateful for this opportunity and many more to come. I give him all the glory, the honor, and the praise.

About the Author

Entrepreneur and author Derrick Taylor is a refreshing new voice to the writing scene. His love for writing emerged after his inspirational journey from the sports world.

He attended Lurleen Burns Wallace Community College in Andalusia, Alabama studying Business and Management. Having experienced success in his ten year professional career in communications, customer training and development, he is now turning his full attention to writing and helping others on the importance of positive change. He spends much of his time mentoring young people through the community and personal venues.

Taylor is in the process of starting his IC-ART Foundation, which encourages and helps youth to reach their dreams of becoming a writer, artist, musician, or any artistic gift they may possess.

Derrick Taylor

Reared in Statesboro, Georgia, Taylor was an outstanding athlete excelling in basketball. He was a two year starter earning numerous awards, one in particular the McDonald's high school All American award, ranking him as one of the best basketball prospects in the nation.

Taylor currently resides in Atlanta, Georgia and enjoys traveling, cooking, spending time with family and of course sports.

Afterword

Dear Reader,

Thank you so much for allowing me to share my story with you. If you would like to arrange for speaking engagements or share your thoughts, please feel free to contact me at DTaylorbooks@yahoo.com. Or visit my website at www.DTaylorbooks.com, where up-to-date information is available. Follow me on Twitter @ TaylortheAuthor.

God Bless,

Derrick

www.ingramcontent.com/pod-product-compliance
Lightning Source LLC
Chambersburg PA
CBHW030320080526
44584CB00012B/647